A Shell Guide

Shropshire

A Shell Guide

Shropshire

by Michael Moulder

Faber & Faber   3 Queen Square   London

First published in 1951
This edition published 1973
by Faber and Faber Limited,
3 Queen Square, London WC1
Printed in Great Britain by
Billing & Sons Limited, Guildford and London
All rights reserved

ISBN 0 571 04755 6

The pictures in these guides are not chosen for their popular holiday appeal, nor as advertisements for the places and buildings they show. The special character of a village or a house or a stretch of country is what, in the end, is exciting and memorable about it, and this character may be brought out not only by camera angles, and quality of negative and print, but by cloud or lack of cloud, in fact by many different effects of lighting, mood, weather and season. These considerations have influenced the choice of pictures more than the demand for conventional compositions in sharp focus and perpetual sunshine.

John Piper

Illustrations

Carving: Feathers Hotel, Ludlow

6

Acknowledgements

Most writers acknowledge the assistance of their wives, "without whom their books would never have been written". This is literally true in this case, for it was my wife who was responsible for much of the initial research and note-taking upon which this book has been based, and who accompanied me on some six thousand miles of exploration. For this I am deeply grateful.

No compiler of a guide such as this can afford to be without the relevant volume of *The Buildings of England*, and I confess that my copy of *Shropshire* is extremely well worn. My thanks then to Professor Nikolaus Pevsner. The previous edition of this book was written by John Piper and Sir John Betjeman, and I am indebted to them for much that has been incorporated from their volume. To John Piper also, as Editor, I am grateful for the opportunity to undertake this book and for his encouragement and helpful suggestions. The Librarians of Shrewsbury, Shropshire and Kidderminster Libraries have been most patient and helpful in my many requests, and to them and their staffs I offer my thanks.

It is impossible to list all the books to which I have referred, but the following have been especially valuable in giving a contemporary view of Shropshire:

R. Gough: *Antiquities and Memoirs of the Parish of Myddle*, 1701
Rev. J. Nightingale: *The Beauties of England and Wales*, vol. 13, 1813
C. Hulbert: *The History and Description of the County of Salop*, 1837
Rev. C. H. Hartshorne: *Salopia Antiqua*, 1841
and, of course, the *Victoria County History* and Dean Cranage's *The Churches of Shropshire*.

In the course of my journeys countless Shropshire folk have helped me with information and given permission to view their houses and take photographs. To the incumbents of the many churches I am particularly grateful in this respect. Mr Bill Dickenson of Ironbridge gave me useful information on Coalport and Caughley wares and kindly lent some original material. Mr W. H. Loads has given unstintingly of his time in meeting my whims in the taking and printing of many of the photographs, and has been a cheerful companion on many visits when the weather has been less than kind. Mrs B. H. Dudley has turned my manuscript into a neat typescript.

For anyone wishing to pursue the study of the industrial revolution in Shropshire there are many excellent books. I have borrowed freely from the following and would like to acknowledge a particular debt to their authors:

T. S. Ashton: *Iron and Steel in the Industrial Revolution*
J. Gloag and D. L. Bridgewater: *A History of Cast Iron in Architecture*
C. Hadfield: *Canals of the West Midlands*
A. Raistrick: *Dynasty of Iron Founders*
L. T. C. Rolt: *Thomas Telford*
J. Plymley: *The Agriculture of Shropshire* which is often quoted by these authors and which contains much that is germane to such a study.

By no means least important is the fine museum at the Coalbrookdale Works of Allied Ironfounders Ltd, successors to the Coalbrookdale Company, and the newly formed Ironbridge Gorge Museum at Blists Hill.

Note. For references to M.P.B.W. in the text read Department of the Environment

Introduction

Belonging

The true Cockney or the "Brummie", the Man of Kent or the Lancastrian all have a strong sense of belonging to a particular town or county. They have their own forms of speech, their own language almost, and above all they have their own name to identify themselves with. So it is with the Salopians. They have their own land and their allegiance to it. No matter how friendly they may be to the visitor, no matter how welcoming to the settler in the county, it is impossible for anyone to become a native by adoption. "I've lived here for forty years, but of course, I wasn't born here." That is the crux of the matter; one has to be *born* a Geordie or Scouser. The English towns, and the counties above all, still have a surprisingly powerful hold on the affections and loyalties of men. A feudal system of land tenure and administration has become so firmly embedded in our way of life that it is almost impossible to conceive of day-to-day living without it. The system itself knits communities closer together, and in the past has accentuated regional and local differences in speech and behaviour, in customs and traditions of building, and often formed the demarcation between contrasting parts of the landscape.

Those boundaries were not inflexible though, and the Shropshire of the Domesday Book was very much larger and included parts of Flintshire, Denbighshire, Merionethshire and almost all of Montgomeryshire. Subsequently, all these districts and the hundreds of Clun, Ellesmere and Oswestry were designated Marches and were hence outside the jurisdiction of the Sheriff of Shropshire. Offa's Dyke is a reasonably accurate guide to the limit of Anglo-Saxon penetration of the wilder western parts of England, and William I, anxious to secure, or at least to stabilise, his boundaries, offered some of his more

◁ Offa's Dyke near Clun

troublesome knights the opportunity to acquire lands for themselves. Whatever they were able to win from the Welsh princes they were to govern as almost independent kingdoms, and three of the greater lordships marcher became palatine earldoms. So the marches (from mark or boundary) were a very important feature of the Border territory, and a virtual wall of castles was built to protect it. Saxton's map of 1577 shows a great clustering of them along the western margins, and in 1627 John Speed was still able to count thirty-two of them. The President of the Council of the Lords Marcher had his seat at Ludlow Castle until the system was abolished during the reign of Henry VIII. In 1535 Clun, Ellesmere and Oswestry were restored to the shire, and the new county of Montgomeryshire was formed out of Caus and Montgomery.

The Landscape

According to the times and attitude of the observer, so the description of the landscape changes. Emphasis is placed on beauty or use, and features are included or omitted as they are seen to add to man's enjoyment (in the widest sense) of the country about him. Thomas Fuller's description of 1663 has nothing romantic about it and is concerned with gaining a living from the land: "A large and lovely county, generally fair and fruitful, affording grasse, grain and all things necessary for man's maintenance, but chiefly abounding in natural commodities." The Rev. J. Nightingale, writing in 1813, adopts a very different viewpoint: "Of the beauties of England, perhaps no county contains a more interesting share than Shropshire; possessing in itself every variety of natural charm: nor is it less rich in the remains of ancient times, awakening reflections, engaging us in the contemplation of memorable events in history." Our point of view today is likely to be

9

no more objective than those of the past, but we can at least say that it embraces something of the romantic, something of the evidence of the "natural commodities" and touching on the "memorable events in history".

The underlying geology inevitably determines the landscape and scenery on the surface in any region, and it is necessary to look at this aspect briefly in order to understand what one sees before one. Simplifying very greatly, the River Severn divides the county in two, flowing first in a south-easterly direction and then swinging south at Ironbridge. The country to the north and east of the river forms the lowland, while south of the river is the great upland area where the rocks break through to the surface.

The Lowlands of the northern plain form a region of gentle slopes, mature, wide valleys with sleepy and slow-moving streams, marshes and meres. The heavier soils make this a rich, green grassland country supporting vast herds of Friesian cattle, black and white to match the half-timbered houses; they supply milk to the cities of the West Midlands. The earth is a warm pink from the underlying New Red Sandstone and it is possible to open a quarry almost anywhere here to obtain a serviceable building stone. Many of the village churches were built of this material, which is quite distinctive in colour, an orange-pink as compared with the pinkish-purple of its relative in the south. At Hawkstone the landscape takes on a more varied character where it rises suddenly from the plain, and Nature has been assisted by man in creating an eighteenth-century landscaped park with an Elysian Hill and Red Castle "curiously ornamented". Not far away, at Grinshill, another more compact and substantial hill is the site of quarries which have provided a better building stone, used for the more important buildings all over the northern part of the county. Otherwise this is a red brick region, and while prosperous agriculturally it presents a rather monotonous picture, relieved here and there by local flashes of beauty or by the excitement of a pleasant building.

The Lowlands of east Shropshire, from Shifnal down towards Bewdley, are more varied, and the valleys of the Worfe and its tributary streams much steeper and more wooded. The lighter and easily worked soils make this an area of arable farming, growing sugar beet for the factory near Wellington, and potatoes, wheat and barley. Between the Severn and the easternmost margins of the Clee Hills is a stretch of country as beautiful as any in the county. Full of swooping and dipping valleys, on the fringe of the Wyre Forest and the former Kinlet Forest, it is known, appropriately enough, as the Wheatland.

The River Severn, "Sabrina fair", enters Shropshire from Wales a few miles below Welshpool and meanders eastward along the margins of the northern plain to where Shrewsbury is almost entirely encircled in its grasp. From there it edges its way through the flat-bottomed valley towards Buildwas with gigantic meanders across the valley floor until it crosses the line of Wenlock Edge. Suddenly the great river comes to life and surges and rushes between the steep and wooded slopes of the Ironbridge Gorge, where in the distant past the waters of ice-dammed Lake Buildwas broke through the barrier of the high ground. Within the gorge the valley sides fall from 400 to 130 feet in less than a quarter of a mile, and this is the most spectacular stretch of the whole river. The famous iron bridge leaps across the gorge in a single span just downstream of the almost sheer cliff of Benthall Edge, and the river plunges on to the companion bridge at Coalport. On either bank in the gorge, climbing up and away, is all the evidence of what was once the birthplace and cradle of the Industrial Revolution. Where once were bustling foundries and forges, lime-kilns and potteries, there is now a peaceful and quietly decaying town with the

above Pennerley, near Shelve ▷
below Snailbeach

Stiperstones

railway lines taken up and only a few factory chimneys still smoking. Industry began, flourished and moved away from here after the coming of the steam engine, which was made possible by the invention and skills of this very place. This is that part of the county where the coal measures lie and stretch up past Wellington. Very few pits are still worked and the ironstone is no longer dug, but the clay is still worked for bricks and tiles, and in Coalbrookdale and further away, up towards Ketley, the tradition of iron working continues. Sad, and only a shadow of its former brightness, this part of Shropshire has a strange beauty about it, where Man's struggle for the "natural commodities" has left an indelible mark.

The Uplands of the south and west lie bounded by the Severn and make not only a marked contrast with the Lowland region but contain, within themselves a rich variety of scenery which is both friendly and intimidating. "The varied landscape is nearly always attractive, the hills high and steep enough to be stimulating, and detached enough to afford glorious views." The character of the upland landscape changes over the four parts of which it is composed. Wildest of all is the district round Shelve, close to the Welsh border and dominated by Corndon Hill across in Montgomeryshire, rising from the surrounding upland with a distinctive rounded cone shape. Skirting the western edge and climbing up and amongst these hills one sees bleak

Long Mynd

and exposed moorlands, scarred and pitted by former lead workings with ruined engine-houses silhouetted against the blindingly white quartzite of the spoil heaps. Perkinsbeach, Myttonsbeach, Snailbeach—and from the last a little mineral railway used to run down to join the main line near Minsterley, carrying lead and slate from the Kelvil Quarry. The tiny loco-shed and some of the track are still there, gradually disappearing into the undergrowth. On and up across rock-strewn moorland are the Stiperstones, which "stand out on the crest of the hill at short intervals like rugged Cyclopean ruins . . .". Jagged and bony against the windy skyline are the Devil's Chair (1647'), and Cranberry Rocks. From the summit the views are superb—to the

south are the Clun Forest hills with Radnor Forest beyond, then Corndon and Long Mountain, and northwards the Breidden Hills and the Berwyn Mountains, with the Shropshire Plain stretched out at one's feet.

Immediately to the east of the Stiperstones is the valley of the East Onny river, green against the bracken of the almost sheer face of the Long Mynd beyond which the upland mass continues. The rocks here are Pre-Cambrian, extremely hard and covered with the thinnest layer of soil, supporting only heather and bracken and spear grass round the boggy pools that form in the depressions in the rock. The more or less level summit rises to 1,696 feet at Pole Bank, and its ten-mile length is traversed

13

by a mediaeval track known as the Portway, a windy but splendid walk at any time of the year, with wonderful views. Towards the southern end gliders of the Midlands Gliding Club soar off the edge to circle over as many as eight counties. Where the hills sweep down towards Church Stretton they are broken up by a series of ravines known locally as "batches", "hollows" and "gullies", each with its own little stream. Carding Mill Valley is the best known and very popular with visitors who make the pilgrimage up to the Light Spout waterfall just below the summit or to the Devil's Mouth. No snobbishness should prevent the reader from seeing this valley simply because it is so popular, for it really is the most beautiful of all. The slopes of these valleys are more hospitable than the plateau, and sheep graze the smooth banks above the streams. The main road from Ludlow to Shrewsbury cuts through Church Stretton on the floor of the rift of that name, which separates the Long Mynd mass from the hog-backed ridges and peaks of the Caradoc Hills, "a mountain range in miniature". From south to north stand Ragleth, Hazler, Hope Bowdler, Caer Caradoc (the highest) and The Lawley, with Hoar Edge behind. The line continues north of the Severn to form the isolated hump of the Wrekin, not an especially high hill (1,334 feet), but seemingly so in contrast to the flat country about it. It dominates the landscape for miles around and has found its way into the folk-lore as the spadeful of earth carried by a giant to dam the Severn at Shrewsbury but dropped here in despair. The local toast to "friends round the Wrekin" is further evidence of the affection in which it is held, and "The Gate of Heaven", "the Gate of Hell" and "The Needle's Eye" (all names of strange rock formations on its slopes) have been incorporated in local legend. From its summit the beacon "streamed in crimson on the wind" to warn of the Armada's approach, for from that point can be seen Snowdon and the Sugar Loaf, Kinder Scout and Rivett Pikes, and a total of seventeen counties.

To the south of the Stiperstones–Long Mynd upland lies the Clun Forest, a continuation of the same mass but separated from it by the valley of the Onny River, and much dissected by its own streams such as the Clun and Kemp rivers, and with the Teme cutting a deeper valley which forms the county boundary. The rock underlying these 1,000-foot hills is the Old Red Sandstone, purplish-pink, hard, and used for most of the older buildings in the region. Although this is called a forest and there are vast plantations of softwood, many thousands of acres are wild moorland inhabited only by sheep. This is the home of the Clun and Kerry breeds, but Shropshires and Suffolks and various cross-breeds are also raised. In autumn as many as 70,000 descend on Craven Arms for the annual sales.

East of these upland masses, Wenlock Edge thrusts its way as a long finger of limestone separating the Clun Forest from the Old Red Sandstone of the Clee Hills. In fact there are two scarps, Wenlock Edge itself, composed of the limestone of that name, and View Edge, a much more broken series of ridges, composed of Aymestry limestone, with Hope Dale dividing the two. This part of Shropshire is probably the best known, in name at least, for this is the land that A. E. Housman wrote of, the part he knew and loved. Well-wooded slopes with beeches and mixed plantations give way to rolling, dusty, yellow-grey fields sown with wheat and barley or green luxuriant pastures for fattening sheep in beautiful Ape Dale or Corve Dale on either side of the Edge. The streams and roads follow the line of the ridge with cool, stone villages scattered along their length, and most of the larger houses are built in limestone too. Quarrying is still an important local industry and the quarries draw a host of fossil hunters seeking trilobites, brachipods and graptolites.

Fringing the limestone to the east is the Clee Hills "plateau", anything but flat, yet a distinc-

◁ *above* Landscape near Hodnet
below The Wrekin from
Wenlock Edge

15

tive region of Old Red Sandstone capped with dolerite, a hard igneous rock known as dhu stone or "Jew stone". Brown Clee Hill, with its twin peaks of Abdon Burf and Clee Burf, and Titterstone Clee dominate the landscape with their bleak and bare slopes dotted with sheep or scarred with vast quarries. The southern slopes of Titterstone Clee command superb views swinging from the very edge of the Black Country right through 180 degrees to the Radnor Forest, and on the summit are the remains of a pre-historic camp. From here the fertile pasture lands and red fields stretch away down to Cleobury Mortimer on the one hand, while on the other lie the tangled hills and slopes dropping down to the River Corve. In this little corner nestle the villages with the prettiest names in all Shropshire: Aston Botterel, Clee St Margaret and Stoke St Milborough, Hopton Wafers and Hopton Cangeford, Hope Bagot and Angel Bank.

Local Style and Materials

Any attempt to describe a local style of building must take into account the two classes of causes likely to have affected that style. T. D. Atkinson set these out so well that it seems sensible to quote his summary: "(1) Those which arose spontaneously from natural conditions such as the available supply of stone and timber and the character of the people; they are likely to extend so far as and no further than the conditions which produced them. (2) Those of more artificial character, concerned with stylistic matters. These are the nicer questions of design; . . ."

What I have tried to do here is to select some aspects of building where there are, or I believe I can detect, local characteristics which mark out Shropshire work. The county forms part of that Border district running roughly north to south along the margin of the uplands which mark the beginning of Wales, and this is significant not only geologically and geographically but also historically. The Border marks the limit of settlement by different racial groups at different times and therefore has a

political and military significance. It has always been a region well endowed with fortresses and castles. The means of ensuring peace caused the region to be subdivided into self-sufficient units which tended to counter-balance any similarities along the north–south line during the early mediaeval period. Again, the feudal system with its hundreds, grouped together into shires (still the basis of our present-day administrative areas), tended to reinforce local differences in style and tradition. It is perhaps these differences which mark out what is a typical Shropshire sandstone church as compared with a Herefordshire example in the same material, and which make Shropshire woodwork rather different from that of Cheshire. However, the boundaries on the western side of the county are those where differences are most marked, and for very good reasons; the Marcher Lordships were separate kingdoms, and even when grouped together maintained a separate identity, different from that of the wilder mountains of Wales and different from the milder plains in the eastern part of the county. When they were abolished the sense of being different remained and traditions were by this time well established. Thus it seems not unreasonable to argue that in this particular instance military considerations created the conditions under which a very local style was able to develop. These remarks apply in particular to the churches in the southern stretch of the Marches, centred on the Clun Forest, where a further factor seems to have operated, namely that of local materials. Although it bears the name forest, this region is at least as much high moorland, yet sufficiently well wooded in the past to have provided all the oaks necessary for building purposes. The pattern of building here by the Normans, after subduing the original inhabitants, was probably that followed by them in most other parts of the kingdom—wooden castles and churches, followed fairly rapidly by more substantial and defensible structures in stone. The "fortress tower" arrangement was used all over the country, but a variation peculiar to Shropshire,

Shrewsbury ▷
p18 The Abbot's House,
Butcher Row,
p19 Grope Lane

and unlike the Worcestershire and Hereford-shire variants, became established fairly early on. Southern Shropshire has an abundance of hard pinkish-grey sandstone (Old Red), and this was employed for the nave and lower part of the towers of the churches. On this base was built the timber-framed belfry or bellcote, which in this part took on a stepped form almost invariably finished with a pyramidal cap. The sides were either covered with vertical boards or plastered over, leaving openings or louvres mainly for the sound of the bells but also for ventilation. (It seems that later replacements of this covering introduced the horizontal boarding.) The towers themselves are squat and quite massive in appearance, the original windows being few and slit-like. A variation on the theme occurs where a very simple Norman church without a tower has been provided with a timber-framed belfry built directly on to the roof itself, as at Ashford Carbonell. This produces a different silhouette but of the same family likeness. There are three examples remaining of the essentially "local" style, at Clun, Hopesay and More, reminders of what must have originated as a hybrid between the earliest Norman timber structures and their later stone counterparts. Border towers these are, with cousins now in the Principality but formerly within the Marches; the low angle of the roof and the feeling of burrowing into the ground for better foothold mark them out as Shropshire churches.

If military requirements and locally available materials gave that particular form to the Border church towers, it was fashion, or style, that gave rise to the development of the timber belfry with a wooden spire above to form a steeple such as is found in other parts of the country with a strong tradition of building in timber. All that can reasonably be claimed for it in "local" terms is a tendency for these to be found in the south of the county and the happy marriage of a wide variety of materials and textures set one against another. Sometimes the contrast is between the size and shape of wooden shingles between belfry and spire as at

Ashford Bowdler, or weather-boarded spire with lead flashing on the angles all set on a tower of Clee Hill stone, as at Ditton Priors. Or even such a rich combination as shingles, vertical and horizontal boarding (with a fancy lead fret) on the slated roof at Bucknell, completed by a vitreous enamelled clock face with a barge-boarded cover for protection. Cleobury Mortimer is famous for its crooked steeple. With all the wooded country round about, it is not surprising that there should be so many steeples in this area south of the Clee Hills.

One other timber belfry must be mentioned, if only for its uniqueness, since it is not especially attractive in itself. This is a little square, shingled bell-tower with white-painted columns and pediments on the red brick church at Minsterley. The church itself is interesting in that it is that rare thing, a building of 1689, built by the Thynne family in a rather naïve version of what was then the very height of fashion. Could it perhaps be that the belfry represents the incorporation of a Border tradition, suitably modernised?

One of the best known and especially typical features of building in the Welsh Marches is the black and white, half-timber type of house which can be found in an almost unbroken chain from Gloucestershire right through to Cheshire. While neither the timber-framed method of construction nor its sprightly black and white "magpie" plumage can be regarded as in any way unique to Shropshire, it does have its own variations on this national theme and the best examples in the county must rank among the best of their kind anywhere. In Saxon times a very large proportion of England was covered with vast forests of oak and there was already a long-established tradition of building in timber throughout the country. This region remained very well wooded long after the forests in other areas had been seriously depleted or had vanished altogether. Looking at the timber-

B

framed houses in Suffolk and Essex today, the stranger might wonder where all that timber had come from, the more so when one realises that the houses remaining represent only a small fraction of those which have been replaced by bricks and mortar. In Shropshire however, and particularly on the western margins, there are still woods and forests, though the trees are now mainly quick-growing conifers with a leavening of older plantations of beech and the oaks and elms of the eighteenth-century parks. The oak was the staple building material here for many hundreds of years, despite the plentiful supply of good building stone, and the tradition died very hard indeed. William Harrison, writing 400 years ago, said "The greatest part of our building in the cities and good towns of England consisteth only of timber, for as yet few of the houses of the communalty (except in the west-country towns) are made of stone". The visitor to Shrewsbury today can still form a very good idea of what an English sixteenth-century town must have looked like, and there are many timber-framed houses and cottages surviving in the country too. Even English oak has a limited life, although it is known to have lasted for at least 900 years in one building, and thus few of the remaining structures are older than the fifteenth century and most belong to the sixteenth and seventeenth. It is important to realise that what we now see as "early" timber houses are in fact quite late, and the products of already fully developed systems of construction.

The earliest remaining type of timber structure is that known as "cruck" construction, where two inward-sloping lengths of timber, or "blades", were joined by a horizontal "tie-beam" or a "collar-beam" at their apex. In their simplest form, such houses had a roof sloping right down to ground level, and the existence of vertical walls is an indication of a more mature form. The cottage at Burlton illustrates very clearly both its own constructional method and ancestry. The notching-in of the purlins on the back of the blades is clearly seen, together with much more recent replacements and renewals, and it would appear that the pitch of the roof may have been flattened somewhat at some stage. The tie-beam supporting the upper floor is not visible in this instance but is presumably covered by the plaster. The feet of the crucks were generally placed on a low stone plinth in these buildings and sometimes the base walls were carried up to first-floor level so that the tie-beam in effect forms a base for the triangle. The house in the Saxon village of Minton takes this form and is particularly interesting in that the three parts of the building clearly illustrate not only the relative ages of the parts but also the immediate increase in floor space and headroom when the box-frame type of construction was adopted. The pitch of the roof changes and would seem too shallow to have ever been thatched, as the cruck portion probably was, although there is a return to a steeper pitch where the gable meets the centre section. One tends to associate cruck construction with cottages, i.e. relatively lowly buildings, but the earliest portion of the Minton house represents a quite substantial building compared with the very crude houses built by the ordinary country dweller. The White House at Aston Munslow appears at first sight to be yet another, but more important, example of a sixteenth-century timber-framed house which was added to first in timber and then in stone, but closer inspection shows it to be much more complicated and much more interesting in its development. Within the sixteenth-century portion are the remains of a cruck-framed hall of three bays, a large house by any standards. Expert opinion inclines to date this part at about 1350, and it becomes clear that crucks were by no means confined to the humbler house. Some light is thrown on both the way in which the house has been altered and also on building methods in this portion by a letter from the owner, Miss J. C. Purser: "Since you were

Cruck construction at Burlton ▷

20

last here we have had numerous repairs done, during which much of the rough-casting on the right hand of the front door has had to be renewed. When the older plaster was removed a framework some 3 in. thick covered with rough hand-cut oak laths was revealed, behind which was the complete untouched building in timber, wattle and daub in perfect condition, exactly as we see it on the kitchen garden side." (Letter from Miss Purser to Mr J. W. Tonkin, Salop. Arch. Soc. Trans. LVIII pt.a.)

Box-frame construction is exactly what the name implies, a close parallel to modern steel framing where the walls themselves carry no load but are simply filled in with windows or

◁ Melverley Church inside
▽ Outside

with such materials as described above. At a later date bricks were used where wattle and daub had formerly served, and sometimes an old infill was replaced in this way. Brick "nogging" of this kind is very common and, where it has not been painted white, makes a contrasting colour combination with the timbers. The Tithe Barn at Hodnet, 1619, is a very good example and also shows very clearly the square panels formed by the posts and beams. This square pattern is very common and in Shropshire, at least, does not appear to be the result of a shortage of timber, but perhaps rather an indication of a wish to keep down costs and the labour involved in all the additional jointing needed by the closely-spaced vertical timber pattern. Certainly there is an example of a building using vertical timbering dating from the fourteenth century (according to F. H. Crossley), at Bromfield Priory, but during the fifteenth century both patterns occur. Finally, in the seventeenth century the vertical patterns can still be found, and so it would appear to be a matter of style and the status of the owner of the house rather than of a clearly defined development from one to the other.

At Melverley is one of the two timber-framed churches in the county, fifteenth or early sixteenth century (the other is at Halston), and this exhibits both forms of construction. Inside, this delightful little church resembles a barn in its structure.

Where the closely-spaced timbers ("post and pan work") were employed there was little need for any bracing, and this is rarely seen in houses of that type in Essex or Suffolk, but where a more open frame was used diagonal braces secure and stiffen the corners. With a square grid as a basis, this soon led to diamond or lozenge patterns, which are more decorative than structural in their intention. The result is much more busy in its effect, making the front of a house rather restless and sometimes almost camouflaging the simple forms of the building. There is an almost infinite series of variations and combinations to be seen in Shropshire—post and pan, square frames with

lozenges or multiple lozenges as at Pitchford, cusps, quatrefoils, ogees and herring-bone, sometimes with almost all of them employed in one building. The later the date the more exuberant the decoration, generally speaking, and the very best examples display marvellous skill in achieving "uniformitie" with "varietie" and not violating the harmony of the whole. The Feathers Hotel at Ludlow is a very well-known instance, with an incredibly rich façade, but there are other less ambitious though equally successful examples such as Bishop Percy's House at Bridgnorth. The intention behind all this decoration was a totally uninhibited desire for ostentatious display on the part of wealthy and successful merchants who had made their fortunes in the wool trade or as clothiers. Fortunately, their pride was matched by the virtuousity and inventiveness of such men as John Abel, 1577–1674, the "King's Carpenter", who worked mainly in Herefordshire but also "framed" the now-destroyed Market Hall at Church Stretton. His epitaph ends:

"His house of clay could hold no longer;
May Heaven's joy frame him a stronger."

Where the timber houses of the eastern and southern counties are often plastered a gentle cream alongside the mellow grey-brown of weathered oak, in the Border counties it has long been the custom to dress them more boldly and the timbers were deliberately blackened. Henry III gave instructions to "repair the walls outside with plaster and to whitewash them", and John Gage, writing in 1822, quotes from the household accounts of Sir Thomas Kytson, 1574: "For plastering and whitening the fare front of my Mr. his house . . . with the blacking of the timber work, xlijs, vjd." The custom of plastering over the whole of the outer wall surface was not generally followed here; where it occurs it is usually a later addition.

Not content with all the splendour of the black-and-white patterning, the Shropshire carpenters, from the fifteenth century, had been in the habit of further enriching the more important

houses with elaborate carving of the corner-posts and bressumer beams and carving and fretting the barge-boards on the gables. The motifs were either tracery and interlacing arcades, as on the Abbot's House in Shrewsbury, or depicted mythical-classical creatures as on the Gatehouse at Stokesay Castle. Barge-boards might be decorated with purely geometric figures or display interlace patterns of vines and scrolls with overtones of a much earlier English tradition. Since they were so exposed to the weather, many of these are replacements of earlier work but some, such as on the church porch at Bitterley, appear genuinely old. At Ludlow, every available surface on the Feathers is carved, even down to the cusps on the front of the upper storey. Wyle Cop in Shrewsbury, and Henry VII's house in particular, is also very rich in carving above street level.

Any substantial timber house in the country almost invariably boasted a porch, often of two storeys as at Old Marton, and sometimes open at ground level as at Woundale Farm, near Claverley. At Pitchford, the present entrance is a very splendid affair with carving and a coved overhang to the louvred top storey which houses a clock and which is capped by a fancifully-shaped gable, thus making three floors in all. The tradition of timber porches is not confined to domestic buildings; the churches have their share and doubtless many of the originals will have been rebuilt in stone. The finest of these is at Munslow, an open-sided structure with beautiful Perpendicular Y tracery and splendid barge-boards. Good seventeenth-century examples can be seen at Worthen and Loppington, where the churchwarden signed his handiwork in 1656.

One other type of timber-framed building must be mentioned—the market hall set on stout posts and open at ground level. This was probably quite a common feature in the towns of Shropshire as in the neighbouring counties;

those at Church Stretton and Bishop's Castle have been destroyed and the only remaining example is at Much Wenlock, where it serves as the Guildhall. This rests at one end on the remains of a stone building but is otherwise supported on oak posts with a very pronounced overhang to the front. The upper storey has closely spaced uprights and two gables to accommodate the very large windows. The borough records refer to it thus: "Upon the 23 & 24 days of this Monethe of September, 1577, was reared the house over the prison house, Mr. Thomas Ludlowe beinge baylif of this town and franches." Upstairs now is the courtroom, very dignified with its Jacobean panelling and royal arms, 1589, and Latin inscription: "This place abhors inequity, loves peace, punishes wrongdoing, upholds the law, honours men of uprightness." Above, proudly, "This worke was done in the time of Master Launcelot Stephens Bailife". But if this type of building has now vanished, it is perpetuated in the stone-built version built by that Wenlock mason Walter Hancock nineteen years later at Shrewsbury.

Whether the building material of house and church was of wood or stone, the roof was invariably timber-framed, and some of those on the churches are particularly good. Most of the usual forms of roof are to be found, but the commonest form is that with collar-beams and arched braces. In the west, towards and along the Border, these are especially pleasing with wind-braces curved to make cusps and quatrefoil shapes. The rafters are close-spaced so that with the purlins the whole inner surface is divided into squares making a series of ribs against the boarding. The structural and decorative treatment is closely related to the timber-framing of the houses of the region, and in some instances the plastering between the dark timbers makes more than an echo of the black-and-white work to be seen outside.

Less a local variation and more in the nature of local examples of a more national style are the very low-pitched, almost flat roofs. These again are divided into panels with the familiar

◁ Two storey porches
above Old Marton Hall
below Woundale Farm near Claverley

cusped braces in between, and with carved bosses where the ribs intersect. The best examples of this type are to be seen at Ellesmere, and St Mary's, Shrewsbury. That over the chancel chapel at Ellesmere has all the features mentioned above, together with beautifully moulded rafters and beams. The fine nave roof at St Mary's is rather later and the bosses there are carved with angels, a pelican and so on. At Eaton-under-Haywood the two types are found together in one church with the collar-beams on arched braces in the nave and, beyond the tympanum, a flat roof with many bosses. Thus the emphasis and richness is placed at the appropriate end of the church and avoids the anti-climax of so many where a splendid nave roof gives on to an indifferent neighbour in the chancel.

Of the domestic roofs it should be noted that where they complete a timber-framed building they are almost invariably of only a moderate pitch, quite satisfactory for tiles and slates but by no means steep enough to sustain thatch. From this it would be unwise to deduce that thatch was not used in Shropshire but only that it had ceased to be common by the time from which most of the remaining timber houses date. There are one or two thatched houses still, a group in Ashford Bowdler near the Herefordshire border and akin to that county's tradition, but otherwise they are so isolated as to form no significant pattern. Again, roof forms are extremely simple and, apart from accommodating cross-wings, I have seen none of the hipped variety associated with half-timbering as is common in the south of England.

Brick. When brick was first used in Shropshire it was a rich man's material, and for more than a hundred years afterwards very substantial houses continued to be built in wood or stone. Plaish Hall is the earliest known brick building, dating from about 1540 and set in magnificent country between Church Stretton and Much Wenlock. Although this is a brick house, it is essentially a rebuilding of an earlier stone house, complete with stone quoins and windows, but with typically elaborate Tudor brick chimneys. Much closer to the ideal brick mansion of the period is Upton Cressett Hall with an imposing gatehouse rather reminiscent of Madeley Court and of similar date. Upton Cressett is contemporary with Plaish Hall but was added to in about 1580 and is altogether a more ambitious building and closer in style to the brick houses and palaces of the south of England. The chimneys are of both the twisted and the star-shaped type and the windows are of brick. As in all the sixteenth-century brick houses in this area, the bricks themselves are red but relieved by a diaper pattern in harder fired blue brick. Whitton Court represents a later development of the Tudor house with a hall and two projecting wings, basically similar to the front of Plaish Hall but on a larger scale and with a centre gable and bay windows. Comparison of these two houses shows just how far and how fast was the movement away from the basic form and how pleasant it was in its variations. By good fortune Whitton Court is open to the public during the summer and it is possible to view this very attractive house at close quarters both inside and out. The climax of this phase of building comes with such houses as Ludstone Hall, bold in design and rich in detail, and very much of their time. Much more vigorous than their more discreet predecessors, these are truly Elizabethan/Jacobean in style and feeling and, at Ludstone, with all the accompaniments of larger windows, stepped and rounded gables and a semi-circular bow-window at the centre. Where the Plaish-style house—E or H plan with traditional angular gables—leads on to more splendid but basically similar houses such as Condover at the turn of the century, there is also the divergence which reached its flowering in Moreton Corbet and such lesser houses as Ludstone. The exuberance and variety of silhouette of the gables in these houses obviously owe much to the influence of the Low Countries, where the brick tradition had extended in a less broken fashion than in England, but in the other elements there is more than a hint of things to come. At Ludstone there is a classical main door with a very ornate head which is even more daring than the gables. Taken with the semi-circular bay-windows on two floors, a motif so close in its detailing as to have surely been borrowed from Kirby Hall, all the elements had been assembled for a second flowering of brick houses. The pattern books of Serlio and de Vries had been well assimilated, and classic elements and their derivatives had become a part of the English vernacular style, in decoration at least.

The next recognisable phase of brick building in Shropshire is that which goes under the name Carolean but where the provincial character of the county is very apparent in the only partial understanding of that splendid style which reached its peak in the work of Wren and his followers. Apart from the stone quoins and pediment, with a more or less elaborate doorway, it is the windows which distinguish the truly refined house of this time. A glance at Soulton Hall, 1668, reveals not only a very incomplete grasp of the more obvious features but retains the older style of window with a shaped gable and rounded pediment on the columns flanking the door.

By 1696 Sir Francis Newport's house at Shrewsbury, now the Guildhall, was not merely a fully developed and excellent example of its type but one very much in the height of fashion. The direct links with the capital bore a rich fruit here and resulted in a house of considerable urbanity. The 12-paned windows with their white-painted frames create a pattern repeated in the Judge's Lodging, 1701, and with the adoption of the flat front make possible the development of the Georgian terrace and street.

Some of the very best townscape in Shropshire stems from this development—the flat-fronted Georgian brick house with trim pedimented doorways or shop fronts below and regular rows of white-painted sash windows above. The terrace as such does not appear, but rows of similar houses, ranging over as much as fifty years and differing in detail, are the making of such towns as Cleobury Mortimer and Newport. There they set the keynote of the High Streets, while in Ludlow, Shrewsbury and Whitchurch they are more widespread and lend charm and dignity to the town as a whole.

Meanwhile, the large country house was changing once more, although it kept the square plan that became popular during the Jacobean period, as at Whitley, near Shrewsbury. John Prince, the self styled "Prince of builders", was the first to introduce this new style to the county at Cound in 1704. Giant pilasters form the frame of the façades, with the windows creating vertical and horizontal rhythms within that pattern. The enormous cornices and parapets cause the roof to disappear from view and for a while the gable vanishes from the more magnificent houses, to be replaced by the pediment. Cound was but the forerunner of a series of splendid brick houses which are either known to be by, or attributed to, Francis Smith of Warwick and which were built between 1726 and 1731. Smith was to be mason to James Gibbs when that architect was building the Radcliffe Camera some six years later, and it can be seen that the local gentry by this time were certainly not disposed to have their houses in a local style in any provincial sense. The link with the mainstream of fashion was firmly established and from this time on was to become increasingly important. Local features and flavours continue to be apparent, but more in the nature of the materials used than in the designs which shaped them. Communications, in all senses, were improving and Shropshire at this time was emerging from its isolation on the Welsh border. It took another fifty years for the roads to become really passable, but ideas and fashions were already abroad and making themselves felt.

Until the nineteenth century, "brick", in Shropshire, can be taken to mean the warm red variety found all over England. In the north and east of the county there are plenty of clays suitable for such bricks and, indeed, plenty of relics of a widespread brickmaking industry. At one time it was common practice for itinerant brick-makers to move about the

St. John's Hill, Shrewsbury

country making bricks from truly local materials, and thus the expense of carrying bulky and heavy loads over inadequate roads was avoided. No doubt this custom was followed in Shropshire as elsewhere, and it seems at least likely that it was so at Upton Cressett, which is in an extremely remote spot and difficult of access. The bricks made and fired under these conditions are of moderate hardness and weather to a very beautiful colour and texture, quite unlike the modern machine-made brick which is harder, harsher in colour and weathers not at all. The earlier bricks were, nevertheless, made under controlled conditions, and some were hard fired to produce the blue-black ends required for making the diaper patterns on Tudor houses such as Plaish Hall or Belswardine Hall.

The earlier buildings, put up as a result of the upsurge of industry in the Coalbrookdale and Madeley areas, are of this same brick, but as the pace quickened the fire-clays found in that area were themselves used for building but especially for the furnaces themselves. The whole of this industrial area is on or close to the coal measures of east Shropshire, and associated with the coal is the fire-clay necessary for the making of linings for the furnaces. Just as a builder of houses opened up a pit for his use, so the Coalbrookdale Company did for their

Broad Street, Ludlow

purposes, and already in 1756 they were able to supply fire bricks at 10s. per thousand and "Brow Brick" at 5s. per hundred for shipping to Monmouth. By 1797 the Horsehay works of the Company were supplying building bricks and fire and furnace bricks for the whole enterprise.

The building bricks made in the Madeley area are quite distinctive and are found only in that area or where they could be easily shipped by river or canal. They are smoky-orange in colour and mottled with great blotches of black, making a richly variegated wall when laid. It is impossible to select or match them for colour, and so the houses and workshops built with them have a warm, dappled appearance which is often set off by white-painted cast-iron window frames or barge-boards. Used only for humbler buildings, they were not carried far and so contribute greatly to the character of an already closely-knit community.

Just as mottled bricks were used for the more lowly buildings, so a different brick was employed for the many churches and chapels or places like the Anstice Memorial Institute in Madeley. The last was constructed of a hard and harsh red brick which is almost vitrified and thus changes not at all. A similar brick was used at Ludlow for the Market there, and the combination of pretentious design with unpleasant material is unhappy in both cases.

29

Madeley: Old Hall

Ironbridge: Tontine Hotel (detail)

The churches and chapels fared much better in both respects and, if not altogether peculiar to this relatively small district, are typical and in keeping with its nature. First there is the so-called white brick, in reality yellow or buff in colour, and much used for the many chapels in Madeley and for the church of St Luke at Ironbridge. Then there is the blue brick, a hard blue-grey material, even in colour and not at all unpleasant when used with stone and white paint. The nineteenth century schools at Bridgnorth and Broseley were built with this brick and it was even used for the incredible gabled front of Dawley Bank Baptist Church.

One of the most inventive uses to which the single-colour bricks were put was in pattern-making on an otherwise plain wall. This custom was not confined to this district, of course, but the local variants were put to good use in this way, especially in building chapels and schools. This polychrome style immediately recalls William Butterfield's experiments on these lines, but the results here are more exotic in form if not in pattern, as can be seen at the Wesleyan Infant School at Madeley Wood (Ironbridge), which is a very lively building, or the New Markets at Bridgnorth, which is terrible. Probably the very best handling is at Dawley, in the Methodist chapel in the High Street, where the combination of colour and relief is extremely well treated.

The use of local clays in building cannot be left without mentioning the tile-making industry, once flourishing at Jackfield, whose best advertisement is Sir Arthur Blomfield's church right outside one of the factory gates. Apart from the ordinary tiles seen all the way up the Gorge from Jackfield there is a rich variety of colour and shape employed on the

Ironbridge

Jackfield

roofs for some distance around and, again, especially noticeable on some of the schools. The roof at Broseley is completed in this way, and the greenish-yellow walls of Norton school (easily taken for a church) are beautifully complemented by the lozenge patterns on the roof. Finally, there are the glazed tiles and bricks also made here and well distributed in the county in the interiors of a variety of buildings.

Stucco. With an abundant supply of good building stone and plenty of bricks at hand, it is not surprising that there should be so few examples of stuccoed buildings in Shropshire. Whereas stucco is often a means of imitating stone where none is available or it is too costly, or as a means of covering an inferior brick, in this county those reasons do not apply. In chapels, where stucco was not uncommon, we find here an un-

ashamed use of brick of various colours, and with the lack of any large housing schemes where appearance was a conscious consideration, there was no occasion for its use. It seems not unreasonable, therefore, to say that where it was used it was for purely aesthetic reasons. The finest example occurs in a country setting where John Nash placed Cronkhill at the top of a hill, backed by trees and with a grand sweep of grass in front. The design is Italianate, asymetrical, with a round tower at one corner and an arched loggia supported on columns running across the front. Round-headed windows echo the circular theme and the walls have recently been renewed in all their gleaming white splendour, so fitting to the design.

Colour, apart from that inherent in the sandstone and bricks of the region, is almost entirely restricted to white. White-painted plaster for the timber-framed houses, contrasting so well

Cronkhill: 18th-century Italianate

with the blackened wood, and the occasional white-painted brick house. Apart from this traditional use of white paint, the obvious reason for its employment is to create a sense of light, and it is thus no accident that it occurs in conjunction with a taste for the classical and Italianate in particular. The railway station at Gobowen is the only other really notable essay in this style, designed with loving attention to detail and remarkably attractive in its fresh white paint. One other instance of the use of stucco, in the Greek manner this time, is the Royal Victoria Hotel at Newport. Attractive in its crispness, it is finished in white and a gentle sage green, with bold, gilded lettering to announce itself.

Stone. Where brick is widespread throughout the county, the use of stone for building falls into a fairly well-defined pattern, and one which relates to the underlying structure. Putting it very simply, north of the Severn is the New Red Sandstone and south of the river the Old Red Sandstone, with the Coal Measures bordering the river to the north and east. Apart from the high ground in the south, these underlying rocks make themselves evident in the rich red soil which Shropshire shares with neighbouring Herefordshire and Worcestershire and on which the pink stone buildings sit so well. Intruding on this pattern of sandstone is the best-known upland in Shropshire—Wenlock Edge—where the limestone breaks through to make a dramatic change in the landscape and to yield a third building stone. These, then, are the elements out of which stone building is compounded here: the Old and New sandstones and the cool grey limestone.

The sandstones of the New and Old deposition, or north and south as they are disposed here, are quite different in character and have a corresponding influence on the style of building. Given a similar design of cottage or church in the two parts of the county there is a marked difference in feeling arising from the different ways of working the stone. Whereas the Old Sandstone is a hard and intractable material, not capable of being cut into regular shaped

Gobowen Station: 19th-century Italianate

blocks, its softer counterpart may be hewn into smooth-faced ashlar and laid with a minimum of mortar. The older rock, by contrast, makes irregular and smaller pieces which need a great deal of mortar and can only be brought into courses with great difficulty and so takes the form of rubble walling with a better stone employed for the dressings. In the earliest churches, where the window openings were small, even this is omitted, and it is only in the later alterations that a free-working stone is brought in for the tracery. One of the ways of handling the smaller pieces of stone in Saxon times was the very attractive herring-bone style of walling which can still be seen at Diddlebury, Culmington and Clee St Margaret. At Diddlebury the whole of the remaining north wall of the nave is built in this fashion. This older stone fractures with an irregular surface, revealing tiny particles of silica which give it a sparkle on close examination and break up the light to give the rock a colder appearance than its cousin to the north. The colours are pink to purplish-red and grey, and in places a brown resembling ironstone.

Laid with a mortar incorporating the local pink sand deriving from the stone itself, the houses and churches of the upland region form a remarkable harmony of colour and texture with the landscape itself. Pink stone blends with pink stone and soil, and forms a pleasant complement to the greener portions, especially when pointed with white-painted barge-boards on the domestic buildings.

North and east of the Severn and away from the uplands of the Clun Forest and the Long Mynd, one is immediately struck by a change in the nature and use of the sandstone. The New Red variety is much hotter in colour, ranging between a purplish-pink and a fierce orange such as may be seen in a number of cuttings alongside the road, and seeming even more intense in the warm light of evening. Fewer domestic buildings are of stone, except where there is a quarry close by, and where stone is used it takes on an importance and significance which is absent further south. Here, it is the churches and grander houses which are built in stone in a region where brick and timber domi-

Cleobury Mortimer

nate and stone is an indication of affluence and social status. The stone can be sawn and cut with a chisel, and although it cannot be too finely carved it wears tolerably well. As a consequence of this, the best carving is found in church interiors such as St Mary's, Shrewsbury, or St Lawrence's, Ludlow, unless, as at Edstaston, a later porch has protected fine Norman carving round the south door.

While the New Red Sandstone forms the underlying rock over most of the country north of the Severn, three quarries have provided the stone for the major buildings there. Two of these were at Highley and Alveley, facing each other across the river near Bridgnorth. The former supplied the stone for part of Worcester Cathedral and the latter that for one of the finest houses in Shropshire, the Prior's Lodge, at Much Wenlock. Here, perhaps more than in any house of comparable size, is a marvellous sense of scale. A series of buttresses divides the wall into bays in a masterly fashion and each

bay is in turn subdivided by the mullions of the gallery windows being carried down to ground level. The result bears some resemblance to the curtain wall of a modern building but is far richer, partly because of the colour and texture of the stone itself but mainly due to the sculptured quality of the wall and the play of light upon it. Sweeping up above is a vast roof, and it is this which, because of its size and uncluttered surface, lends scale and grandeur to the house. The roof is clad with stone slates which gradually diminish in size towards the ridge and add variety of texture to the whole. Such "slates" are common in Much Wenlock and come from the old Hoar Edge quarry a few miles away; they were used also at Pitchford Hall and Madeley Court and are, of course, of sandstone, not limestone as in the Cotswolds.

The other important quarry was at Grinshill, an outcrop rising to almost 450 feet in flat country between Wem and Shrewsbury. Now long-abandoned as sources of building stone, the "red" quarry at the foot of the hill and the "white" quarry at the top supplied excellent stone for the Romans at Uriconium and, many centuries later, for such buildings as Attingham and St Chad's, Shrewsbury. The red variety ranges through pinks to brown while the white is really a greenish-grey.

The great impetus towards the full exploitation of the cutting qualities of the New Red Sandstone in domestic architecture came only with the Jacobean era when the "prodigy houses" were being built and were influenced by the ideas flooding in from Italy at that time. In spite of this, however, it was still possible for the timber-framed Pitchford Hall to be built at the same time as Moreton Corbet and for the same reason —sheer pride and ostentation. But Condover followed in 1598 and firmly established stone as superior to timber for the man of consequence for the next fifty years. The new Market Hall in Shrewsbury was built by the man who probably built Condover, and in 1595 Sir Francis Newport wrote to the bailiffs of the town; "Whereas I am enformed that you intend to buyld a new market house of stone in that towne and so go forward with the work next spring, I pray you let mee comende a Mason of approved skyll and honestye, one Walter Hancock, unte yo for the doing thereof . . .". One may reasonably suppose that the earlier building was in timber and that the bailiffs were bringing things up to date. But fashion was to swing away from stone quite rapidly, and by 1650 brick was coming into vogue and was not to be ousted for almost a hundred years for building in the grand manner.

The Palladian style did not reach Shropshire until 1742, at Linley Hall, by Henry Joynes, and even then it did not have very much influence. It was not until James Wyatt rebuilt Badger Hall, 1779–83, and George Steuart designed Onslow House in 1780, that the second great phase of building in stone commenced and the fine-grained Grinshill stone came into its own once more. Three years later Steuart's Attingham Park was begun and, the structure at least, completed some two years later.

Robert Mylne's Aston Hall is yet another example of this apparently sudden urge towards the classic design, much simpler than anything which had gone before and demanding smooth surfaces to reflect the light and allow form to take precedence over ornament. Shropshire had by this time emerged from its relative isolation, and through its landowners and patrons of the arts it was swept into the eighteenth century and so caught up with styles and fashions originating in Bath and London. Robert Adam's influence was felt through the work of Wyatt, Mylne and, especially, Steuart, whose output was not great but certainly imaginative and without it the county would be very much the poorer. It is a pity that his Onslow House and Lythwood Hall have been destroyed, as also Wyatt's Badger Hall, but his two churches remain to demonstrate his stature and provided a model for Telford shortly after.

The best town houses in Shropshire are either timber-framed or in red brick, and since there is no example of either eighteenth- or nineteenth-century town planning, there are very few houses consciously related to each other. One notable exception to this, albeit on a small scale, occurs in Shrewsbury in Claremont Bank where there is an early nineteenth-century terrace of stone houses by Carline and Tilley, ashlar faced. It seems a pity that the many good buildings of this and a slightly earlier period could not have been grouped together to give more of this character to this pleasant but rather untidy part of the town. Perhaps if Nash had been as active in the town as he was in the country the picture would be different today.

In the folded uplands south of the Severn the ridges lie like a hand spread out with the long pointing finger of Wenlock Edge as one of the best-known features of the English landscape. The rock here is limestone, of two sorts, the Wenlock below with the Aymestry stone above it. The Priory here, "the oldest and most privileged, perhaps the wealthiest and most magnificent, of the religious houses of Shropshire", was built largely with the local grey stone and very splendid it is, even as a ruin.

The stone is capable of being dressed into blocks and some will even take a fair degree of polish; it is known as Shropshire marble. It withstands the weather well, better than the New Red Sandstone, but is found only within fairly closely defined limits near its source. This stretch of country embraces Wenlock Edge itself, with Ape Dale and Corve Dale on either side, and has all the typical features of limestone country; in parts it is reminiscent of the Cotswolds. The contrasting configurations of the landscape itself and the different colour and texture of the stone here provides a welcome relief from the otherwise universal red soil and pink stone churches. Within this small compass are some fine stone houses—Wilderhope Manor, a gabled house of 1586, and, of almost identical date, Shipton Hall with an elegant Georgian classic stable range in front. At Morville, to the east, is another Elizabethan house, but almost entirely rebuilt in 1748–9 in a classical style. There are two projecting wings linked by curved walls to the service ranges which are topped with delightful gilded cupolas and elaborate ironwork. The scale here is quite modest and results in one of the pleasantest houses of its kind in the whole of Shropshire. At Cleobury Mortimer, away from the main limestone region, is an unpretentious stone house opposite the church which gives a clue to what may be found in the town. Tucked away behind the church is a fine stone building with a hipped roof and lantern and excellent pedimented doorway. This is Childe's School, 1740, another example of that little awakening in stone in the mid-eighteenth century and for which the cool coloured limestone seems so appropriate.

The Clee Hills are the only other notable source of stone, but it is of little use for building and is employed chiefly for road making. In the nineteenth century, some of the "dhu stone", or Clee Hill marble as it is sometimes called, was used at Hopton Court nearby, but this was an exception and its only other use was in the quarrymen's cottages round about.

During the nineteenth century there were rather fewer grand houses built in the county and of those that were built their significance lies more in the change and variety of style than on the use of local materials. This tendency had been growing throughout the previous century and after 1800 building in stone took on a cosmopolitan rather than a local flavour. Where brick flourished, stone progressively dwindled, though some fine houses were built for the wealthy during this century. Longner Hall, 1803, by John Nash, is the sole remaining example of his exotic and assymetric Tudor style, and although Repton disagreed about its siting it remains a delightful Gothicky house. Willey Hall, by Lewis Wyatt, about 1816, is firmly Greek Revival in style and supremely well sited above a chain of lakes. Millichope Park, 1840, by Edward Haycock of Shrewsbury, continues in the same tradition, also superbly sited by water, where Wenlock Edge drops away to Corve Dale. By 1879 fresh ideas were abroad and Norman Shaw's Adcote reflects his ability to borrow from the English tradition and yet design in a creative and imaginative manner.

The Church Towers

To attempt to summarise the development of church building in Shropshire in a few pages would be either presumptuous, since Dean Cranage spent half a lifetime on the subject, or impossibly tedious if condensed to a mere table of facts and dates. To describe some of the more interesting towers, however, will be to illustrate some of the more important and rewarding features of that development, leaving the reader to fill in the gaps for himself. Obviously, towers are by no means always contemporary with the rest of the church which they grace, and it would be safe to say that the majority have had their battlements added or renewed, yet they convey in a small compass the range and flavour of Shropshire church building.

Of the earliest known towers of the Norman era very little remains and none of the remaining work can date from much before 1100. The different types of stone and the different circumstance as regards security are reflected and result in different styles within the county. The "fortress towers" of the Border have already been described with their squat proportions and un-dressed stone, topped with a wooden belfry, but further east a more sophisticated style was possible. This was due in some measure to the greater security of the region, but the less intractable type of sandstone lent a certain grace where robustness was otherwise the essential quality. The more or less complete Norman church at Linley, near Broseley, is typical of this more relaxed style. In Shrewsbury, at St Mary's, one sees a similar pattern but on a grander scale and with the dignity and refinement one would expect in a town of this size and importance. The upper parts and spire, one of the tallest in England, are in the Perpendicular style. A similar comparison may be made between the towers of Lydbury North, again near the Border, and Much Wenlock parish church. Both belong to the early thirteenth century but with later battlements, and again there is the marked contrast of style and material. This is Transitional architecture, but in a sense the transition never took place, or was so gradual that there is not very much to which one can attach the label Early English. Much Wenlock Priory is sadly ruined, but it is there and at St Mary's, Shrewsbury, that the wealth of this style lies; if one insists on the tower theme, then it is necessary to turn to Shifnal or Kinlet. Market Drayton and Newport represent the earlier part of the fourteenth century, preparing the way for the splendours of the next hundred years and with a fine and massive example at Alberbury and an unusual detached octagonal tower at Hodnet. Possibly one of the best of the simpler towers in the Perpendicular style is that at Upton Magna, very dignified in its carefully dressed stone and looking out over the flat country near the Severn. Most splendid of all, though, is Ludlow, a crossing tower built in about 1470 and so tall that it dominates not only the town but also the country all about. This is what a church tower ought to look like, and if ever Shropshire were to have a cathedral of its own there could be only one other contestant for that privilege. In complete contrast is the crossing tower at Tong. It starts on a square base which changes to an octagon complete with pinnacles and is completed by an octagonal spire. The silhouette is very attractive and unique in the county and yet perhaps it may owe something to the tower at Hodnet. Greatly enriching the skyline of Shrewsbury are the sister spires of St Alkmund's and St Mary's.

Normally one would expect something of a break at this point but there was a surprising amount of church building, or more precisely, rebuilding, going on in Shropshire during the seventeenth century. The style was not exactly forward-looking, with the possible exception of Minsterley, but if the belfry there may be taken as an apology for a tower, one sees not only brick being employed for the first time but an acceptance of, and an attempt to work in, a wholly contemporary style.

By 1712, at Adderley, one is quite clearly witnessing the beginnings of a completely new era of church building and one embracing a different spirit, and in St Alkmund's, Whitchurch, of the same date, one sees already a mature embodiment of that spirit. All the elements of the Georgian church are present—the round-headed bell openings and circular windows, a balustrade with urns and pinnacles where before there had been battlements. It has its counterparts on a humbler scale in the red brick towers of Chelmarsh, Great Bolas, Quatt and Church Pulverbatch, and very attractive they are. The next move came with George Steuart's All Saints at Wellington in 1790, where the tower springs from, but is subordinate to, the nicely proportioned classical west end of the church. While paying homage to the English tower tradition, this one does not have the sureness of the rest of the church. Ten years later, at St Chad's, Steuart solved the problem by abandoning the square except as a base for the octagonal and circular stages above. He had almost certainly been studying the work of James Gibbs, but it is interesting to see how at Tong a similar progression had been adopted but with a spire instead of the circular stage. At the time when St Chad's was being completed, Telford was involved in a similar problem at St Mary's, Bridgnorth, and although the result makes an indispensable contribution to the town as a whole it is quite clear that Telford was a better engineer than he was architect.

By a strange chance, at the moment that Steuart brought the classical movement in the county to a great point of achievement, the swing back to a revival of the Gothic style was beginning in the rebuilding of the nave of St Alkmund's, scarcely a mile away. The pendulum swung between the Grecian and the Gothic for a short while, but "Christian" architecture won and the result was the lancet style of Ironbridge, 1836, in yellow brick by Thomas Smith of Madeley. This is severe in style but wholly in keeping with its surroundings and making superb counterpoint with the bridge below. Haycock's Cressage tower in the same style has a strange papery thinness about it despite the use of stone, and it is not until Benjamin Ferrey's Chetwynd in 1865–7 that one finds an architect creating within the Gothic style rather than merely recreating. The tower is placed assymetrically and is covered with a tall broach spire, a pleasant echo of earlier Shropshire traditions by an architect who did quite a lot of work in the Border counties. Of about the same date but vastly different is Blomfield's Jackfield, which is a turret rather than a tower, and might be regarded as a warning rather than as a model, whatever the merits of the rest of the church. Finally, at Batchcott in 1891, Norman Shaw reverts to a simple but inventive use of small stones within a design which has something of the breadth of the late Norman work of the Border churches.

Iron. In a county so deeply involved in the history of the iron industry, especially from the eighteenth century onwards, it is inevitable that iron should figure very largely. The tradition of ironmaking goes back a very long way here, and an example of the early use of wrought iron in connection with building is the hinges of the door at Edstaston church, believed to be contemporary with the Norman doorway itself.

There are other examples of this kind, but the next obvious use of wrought iron occurs in the entrance gates to a number of the grander houses. These all belong to the eighteenth century but can be divided into two groups—those of the early part of the century where the smith's art is expressed in flowing, wreathing lines like the tendrils of a plant, and with the same sense of growth, and those of the latter part of the century, where the designs are essentially geometric, though equally good of their kind. Robert Adam's influence is very evident in the gates of the magnificent screen at Attingham, while the earlier style can be seen at Preston upon the Weald Moors Hospital and Peplow Hall. At Berwick Hall chapel there is a good and rather uncommon eighteenth-century communion rail in wrought iron.

Cast iron formed the basis of the prosperity of the industrial communities in Shropshire during the eighteenth and nineteenth centuries and was at first used in lieu of other materials but was also used in its own right, the two going hand in hand and occurring simultaneously. The most widespread and most obvious use of cast iron is in the manufacture of window frames to be seen all over the county. The designs varied from the standard round-headed pattern, very commonly used for factories and workshops, and chapels too; the same design is used by Steuart in St Chad's and at Wellington. More elaborate versions include lancet designs, and at Adderley a complete system of tracery was produced for the rebuilding of the church in 1800. Closely related are the fanlight designs seen in many Georgian door heads. Outside, cast iron was used for highly decorative porches, as at Wrockwardine, and for railings and gates.

Apart from these decorative, though functional, purposes, cast iron was employed instead of wood or stone for columns and pillars, and the little church at Tilstock, 1835, is interesting for the degree to which iron was used there.

Cast-iron:
St. Chad's Shrewsbury ▷

Not only was it used for the windows but also for the gallery railings and supports; it was the spanning of the columns with iron which had such significance in Shrewsbury some forty years previously. Iron beams had been used in constructing a multistorey building in the early 1790s, but it was not until 1796 that Charles Bage designed a flax-spinning mill at Ditherington, just outside Shrewsbury, which used both iron columns and beams and thus became the first iron-framed building in the world. The structure was still concealed within brick walls but it was not long before the frame was moved to the outside as in its timber-framed ancestors and was revealed for all to see. A late example of this can be seen in Messrs Birchall's shop in the High Street at Whitchurch, very neatly finished in black and white.

Equally significant in terms of the structural use of cast iron is the famous iron bridge which gave its name to the "mercantile part of Madeley" in the Severn Gorge. Abraham Darby's 100-foot span over the Severn in 1779 was the forerunner of all iron bridges, but apart from its historical importance it is one of the most beautiful bridges in the country. Buildwas bridge, designed by Telford and also made at the Coalbrookdale works, followed in 1796, but spans a full 130 feet with less than half the quantity of iron. Although there remains only a fragment of that bridge, those at Cound and Coalport are still preserved as further evidence of the tremendous importance of the work of the Darbys.

Wherever you go in Shropshire it is hard to get away from iron. The mile-posts are made of it and many of the sign posts also, and then at journey's end, the very tombstones too.

Monuments and Memorials

Memorial brasses have for a long time been regarded as worthy of scrutiny but, through the Victorian custom of taking rubbings, have tended to become collectable items rather than artifacts to be judged critically. It happens that Shropshire has very few pictorial brasses and if

this is not too morbid a pastime, one is forced to look for other forms whereby man's memory has been perpetuated. If one sets aside the sculptor's and monumental mason's contribution in the form of effigies, one is forced actually to read what was said of people and to consider the way in which it was written or carved. This is well worthwhile in any county and what is found here has its counterpart in many other places. Nevertheless it has given me a great deal of pleasure to seek these things out and so I may perhaps be forgiven for drawing attention to what is so obvious yet undervalued if the condition of many of the examples is anything to judge by.

The tombstones in Shropshire churchyards before the invasion by incongruous white and black marble were almost entirely of red sandstone or limestone and naturally blend well with the surrounding walls and the church itself. Given a few years to acquire a degree of weathering and a crusting of lichen they complete a very English scene. The standard of letter-cutting never reached any dizzy heights, but up to the early years of the nineteenth century was usually quite respectable and sometimes very good. Wherever there was a good craftsman at work one sees an immediate impact on the stones in that churchyard, as at Lilleshall, in spite of the way in which it has been despoiled. Sometimes there is a surprisingly late survival of the best standards, as at Chirbury, or a strong tradition of the double-headed stone as at Selattyn. Table-tombs are common in the eighteenth century and often include some pretty decoration as well as fine letter-cutting, and just occasionally there is a brass plaque let into the stone to bear the inscription. These local stones do not weather very well, and when set up on edge the frost eventually attacks them and they begin to flake away, so it is unusual to find many of the charming seventeenth-century angels and cherubs of that time. Much more enduring are the cast-iron head-stones, table-tombs and more elaborate plinths with urns on top and railings to protect them. These were painted when new but most have settled to a pitted rusty brown or black. Logically enough these are found mainly

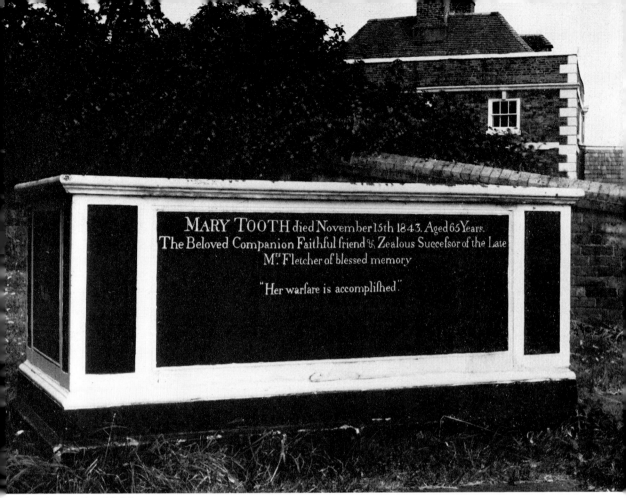

Cast-iron tomb at Madeley

in the Dawley and Madeley area, and Madeley churchyard is the richest spot of all. Iron is not restricted to the outside of the churches, however, for at both Leighton and Bridgnorth there are seventeenth-century ledger slabs, presumably made at the foundries in those places.

Within the churches there is a remarkably good range of memorials, and though brasses are few there are some very good fifteenth and sixteenth century ones at Tong to the Vernon family, showing the dress of the period. The seventeenth- and eighteenth-century brasses at Oswestry and Child's Ercall consist of an inscription only, but the quality of the lettering and layout there put many of the later craftsmen to shame. At Clungunford the brass was set in a wooden frame carved and painted to simulate marble. Allied to the more usual memorial brasses are the magnificent alabaster slabs found at Pitchford, Beckbury and Claverley, often as much as six feet long and incised in the same manner as brasses but with the lines filled in with pitch. There is usually a border formed by a black-letter inscription and rows of kneeling children fill the place otherwise occupied by the lion or dog. Ranging from the late fifteenth to the end of the sixteenth century, they provide a charming guide to Tudor costume. At Greete, Wentnor, Edgton and Onibury there is a variation on the carved tablet where the background has been lowered and the surface painted black, making a welcome relief to the more conventional tablets. Slate is uncommon but there are notable examples of its use at Bettws-y-Crwyn and Eaton-under-Haywood. This latter church is certainly the richest in the whole of Shropshire in its wealth of tablets which yet do not overpower and add greatly to the character of the interior. On the wall outside, next to the porch, is a splendid eighteenth-century tablet to one Stephen Oxenbold, with a neat little frame and pediment above. The custom of fixing tablets to the outside walls occurs also at Stoke St Milborough, where the east wall of the chancel is covered with them.

Shropshire is rich in effigies carved in alabaster, painted and gilded and often set on a canopied tomb further enriched with colour. Tong and Kinlet excel above all others in the sumptuousness of their collections, but Wroxeter and Moreton Corbet rival them in quality if not in quantity. They spread over almost 200 years, from the end of the fifteenth to the beginning of the seventeenth centuries, and are in remarkably good condition. There are also isolated examples scattered over the county, the Cotton monument at Norton-in-Hales for example, and the Conyngsby monument at Neen Sollars. Towards the end of the seventeenth century the figures on the tombs are more upright and there is a strong move to naturalism. Colour is no longer used and the feeling is more of what is generally expected of sculpture. There is a pleasant example at Quatt, 1678, and by 1746 the style is fully exploited in two figures by Roubiliac at Condover. Badger church contains works by three of the best-known English sculptors of the early nineteenth century—Flaxman, Chantrey and John Gibson—and continue the tradition of patronage which caused Wyatt to design the now demolished Hall there.

The Industrial Revolution

The essence of the industrial revolution in Shropshire lay in two related events or sequences of events, with the Darby family and the Coalbrookdale Company providing the link between them and the people responsible for them. Abraham Darby moved in 1708 to Coalbrookdale, an area where there was already a long-established iron industry, and by early 1709 had perfected the smelting of iron with coke. This was of fundamental importance since the English forests had been so plundered for charcoal making that supplies of fuel were inadequate to meet the demand for iron goods. The staple output of the works at this time was cooking pots and other smaller items, and this continued alongside all the subsequent production in other fields. In 1712 Newcomen constructed the first effective steam engine, or "that surprising machine for raising water by fire", as *The Morning Chronicle* described it, to operate a pump at Dudley Castle. This and subsequent engines had cylinders cast in brass, a very costly business, but by 1722 iron cylinders were being cast at Coalbrookdale far more cheaply. Not only was the cost less, they could be made much larger and thus of a greater value since they were relatively inefficient machines. Twenty years later there appears the first record of a steam engine being employed in the works themselves, to operate a pump, and many more were built for this purpose and to provide a draught for blowing the furnaces in the various parts of the Dale. The Company continued to produce engines for its own use and both cylinders and complete engines for sale outside. James Watt, meantime, had taken out patents for an engine where the movement was converted to a rotary action and, with his entry into partnership with Mathew Boulton in Birmingham, he was able to produce a really efficient engine which also incorporated Watt's other innovation of a separate condenser. Boulton & Watt supplied one of these to the Darbys' main competitor, Wilkinson, in 1782, to power his forge hammers, and the Darbys followed in the same year, installing one in their Ketley works. One of the main obstacles to the building of first-class engines had been the impossibility of machining accurately the insides of the cast cylinders, but with the invention of Wilkinson's boring machine this problem was overcome. As Mathew Boulton put it: "Wilkinson hath bored us several cylinders almost without Error; that of 50 inches diamr for Bentley & Com doth not err the thickness of an old shilling in no part."

Richard Trevithick had meanwhile been developing his ideas for a steam carriage, after perfecting for the first time a high-pressure engine which required only a small cylinder. This brilliant young man was familiar with the Coalbrookdale engines through his experience as an engineer in the Cornish mines and he quite naturally turned to the Dale Company for assistance with his "carriage". In 1802 he wrote from Coalbrookdale reporting on its progress: "The say it is a super-natureal engine for it will work without either fire or water, and swears that all the engineers hitherto are the biggest fools in creation. They are constantly calling on mee, for the all say its an imposiabelity, and never will believe it unless the seeit . . . but after a short time the setts off with a solid countenance and a silent tongue. . . . The Dale Co have begun a carriage at their own cost for the realroads and is forcing it with all expedition." The experiment was a success, and so the world's first railway locomotive was born. It seems very likely that the drawings in the Science Museum refer to the locomotive built by and for the Coalbrookdale works in 1802 rather than to the Pen-y-Darran machine, which seems to have come from Hazeldine's Foundry at Bridgnorth and which certainly built Trevithick's Catch-me-who-Can of Euston fame.

In his letter, Trevithick takes for granted the "realroads" existing in the works, but these had undergone fundamental changes not many years earlier. Wooden rails had been in use for wagons carrying coal from the mines in the late 1600s, but it was not until 1748 that they were employed within the iron works. Richard Reynolds, who had taken over the Company's Ketley works in 1756, began replacing the wooden rails in about 1767 with ones made of cast iron, and by 1785 over 20 miles had been laid, linking the Ketley, Horsehay and Coalbrookdale works, and the Company's wharves on the Severn. These were the world's first iron rails, and were one personally involved it would seem like boasting to record yet another first, because in 1779 Darby had designed and built the world's first iron bridge. But this is an attempt at an objective recording of facts, and the facts are that this tiny valley of Coalbrookdale and its immediate neighbourhood were responsible for, or involved in, a remarkable number of discoveries and innovations fundamental to the industrial revolution in England and hence in the world. This was due largely to the inventiveness and imagination of the Darby family and their Quaker associates and their highly successful business. They established a wide range of contacts throughout industry and the engineering world, and their receptiveness to new ideas and willingness to undertake experiments resulted in the achievements upon which modern industrial society is based. In paying tribute to the Darbys and the Coalbrookdale Company the contribution of that other great iron-master, John Wilkinson, must not be ignored. So single-minded was he in his love for iron that he made an iron coffin for himself and, to mark it, an iron obelisk, still standing in Lindale, Lancs. His main contributions were the boring machine used so effectively for the machining of engine cylinders, but also for cannon, and the first iron boat, which was launched at Willey Wharf on the Severn.

The invention of the railway locomotive presaged a great expansion of communications during the nineteenth century, but during the last quarter of the eighteenth century industry and manufacture were growing faster than the means of distributing the products. Brindley's first canal for the Duke of Bridgewater was opened in 1761, and the rapid expansion of this new form of transport gave the Shropshire ironmasters an easier and cheaper route to the north. The Severn had been their chief outlet until then and so it continued to be for many years to come. In the early part of the nineteenth century the Severn was reckoned the busiest river in Europe, save only the Meuse, and Hulbert records: "perhaps 150 vessels on the river [at Coalport] actively employed or waiting for cargoes". It is no surprise to find that Brindley was a customer and well known at the Coalbrookdale Works, and that Richard Rey-

nolds there became convinced of the possibilities of a canal system. His son William was responsible for making a towing path for horses from Coalport to the iron bridge where men had previously been employed in what Telford described as "barbarous and expensive . . . slave-like" work. In 1788 an Act was obtained to allow "a navigable canal from the principal iron works in Shropshire to the river Severn", and it was William Reynolds who was largely responsible for its design and its most striking feature, the inclined plane. Thomas Telford describes how Reynolds overcame the problem of the great discrepancy in height between the two levels at Ketley: "he made a navigable canal, and instead of descending in the usual way, by locks, continued to bring the canal forward to an abrupt part of the bank, the skirts of which terminated on a level with the iron works. At the top of this bank he built a small lock, and from the bottom of the lock,

and down the face of the bank he constructed an *inclined plane* with a double iron railway. He then erected an upright frame of timber, in which across the lock, was fixed a large wooden barrel; round this barrel a rope was passed, and was fixed to a moveable frame; this last frame was formed of a size sufficient to receive a canal boat, . . . This frame was placed in the lock, the loaded boat was also brought from the upper canal into the lock, . . . upon the lower gates being opened, the frame with the boat, passed down the iron railway, on the inclined plane, into the lower canal, which had been formed on a level with the Ketley iron-works, being a fall of 73 feet." From this beginning the whole of the country east of Shrewsbury and north of Coalport became criss-crossed with canals, with the Shrewsbury Canal itself eventually linking up with the Birmingham and Liverpool Junction via the Newport Branch. In 1787 Thomas Telford was appointed Surveyor of Public Works for Shropshire—"I lay the Town and Country under Contribution in every direction (only in the building line) . . ." and was

◁ The Canal at Grindley Brook
▽ Canal Warehouses at Ellesmere

to make a great impact on the county. During his term of office he was responsible for the building of no fewer than forty bridges and, of course, the making of the Holyhead Road. Apart from this he designed three churches and worked on Shrewsbury Castle and the County Gaol. It was not long before he visited Coalbrookdale, and his first iron bridge (at Buildwas) was cast there in 1795. In the same year Telford was appointed "General Agent" to the Ellesmere Canal Company, and on 13 March wrote: "I have just recommended an aqueduct of iron, and it will be executed under my direction." This was the iron trough for Longdon-on-Tern which, if not the first of its kind, was completed only one month after that on the Derby Canal; the iron work was cast at Ketley. Again the same year, 1795, Mr William Jessop reported: "I must now recommend to the Committee to make this saving by adopting an Iron Aqueduct [Pont-y-Cysyllte] at the full height originally intended . . . 125 feet above . . . the River Dee . . . the arches . . . of the Aqueduct may be seven of 50 feet each the remainder may be raised by an embankment." Telford was to draw up the plans. In the meantime, however, work went ahead with the Chirk Aqueduct with iron bottom plates supplied by William Hazeldine. Chirk is on the border of the county, and Pont-y-Cysyllte is a few miles into Denbighshire, but it is so much part of the Shropshire story as to be reason for including mention of it here. Telford considered "that no serious difficulty could occur in building a number of square pillars, of sufficient dimensions to support a cast iron trough", and so the great acqueduct was completed and opened in 1805. How the credit for this achievement should be shared between Jessop and Telford is not altogether clear, but the work remains as one of the greatest engineering feats of the canal age. Telford was later appointed engineer to the Birmingham and Liverpool Canal, running on a line just to the east of the county boundary but crossing into our territory just north of Norbury Junction, near Newport. This, the Ellesmere Canal, and all the small canals were joined to form the Shropshire Union and thus incorporated "in one system the alpha and the omega of Telford's engineering career."

Telford

In 1965 a plan was published showing the outlines of the New Town proposed for the Dawley–Madeley area and to be known as Dawley New Town. The name has subsequently been changed to Telford, and there are proposals for the Wellington–Oakengates complex to be incorporated in the development. This new town differs from most others of its kind in that it has, perforce, to accommodate long-settled communities such as Madeley, Dawley and Ironbridge and to develop new housing and industry without violating the strong character of those existing towns. As a result, the New Town will consist of a number of smaller groupings within a unified whole, each being to a degree self-sufficient but with a new town centre at Randlay Lake. Ironbridge, Coalbrookdale and the Severn Gorge are to be treated as a conservation area of special architectural and historic interest, and a unique open-air museum has been set up at Blists Hill, preserving and displaying the industrial past of the area. A great deal of landscaping has already been carried out and the residential areas of Woodside and Sutton Hill are complete. Whether subsequent development will improve upon these from a visual standpoint, as additions to an area with outstanding possibilities, remains to be seen. So far, the result is bitterly disappointing.

Gazetteer

The number after each entry refers to the square on the map following page 152 where the place is situated

Abdon (14). The village itself is 800 ft. up. Towering above it, the bracken- and gorse-covered but treeless slopes of Abdon Burf rise almost another 1,000 ft. to Brown Clee's summit. Nordy Bank camp looms high to the south. Scattered hill farms and cottages spatter the hill slope, and larks and grouse populate the thick heather; sheep graze where they can. The views across to Wenlock Edge and down into Corvedale are very fine and it is the setting here that is so splendid rather than the village itself. The best approach is up from Tugford, following a brook shaded with elm, ash and holly, to the Victorian church and tiny school.

Acton Burnell (11). Set in a wooded valley, the village has a prosperous and well-cared for appearance. The Castle of Robert Burnell, Bishop of Bath and Wells and sometime Lord Chancellor to Edward I, is now only an interesting and well-maintained battlemented shell (M.P.B.W.). There is no trace of the "greate barn" (Leland), in which Edward I's Parliament met in 1283 and passed the Statuum de Mercatoribus ("The Statute of Acton Burnell"), which ordained that all debtors in London, York and Bristol should meet their respective mayors and fix a date for payment, on penalty of confiscation of their property. Eventually the castle passed into the hands of the Smythes, a Roman Catholic family.

Acton Burnell Hall, which replaced the castle as the home of the Smythes, is an elegant, though unostentatious, Georgian-style stuccoed mansion with an Ionic portico of stone under which is the carriage entrance. It is surrounded by lawns, shrubberies and a fine deer park, with two lakes amid a low hilly landscape. A ruined Gothic house on a little mound overlooks the artificial lakes, which are well stocked with wildfowl. Adjoining the house is the R.C. domestic chapel, built by refugee French monks in the eighteenth century.

The church is E.E. in the cruciform plan but has been considerably ruined by the "restoration" which demolished the pews and tore up the pavement. There is a square leper's window to the left of the altar and some fragments of a diaper-pattern fresco. The roof is black and white and there are several examples of Jacobean carving. The brass of Nicholas de Handlo, 1382, is very fine and the N. transept contains some good eighteenth-century monuments to the Smythe family, especially the unique tablet of 1764 with marble cross, also the particularly sumptuous canopied tomb of Sir Richard Lee, d. 1591.

ACTON BURNELL

A pretty little Gothic gatehouse stands near the church and there is plenty of decorative cast iron to be seen in the village. An attractive row of nineteenth-century black and white cottages with ornate barge-boards leads towards the unusually elegant school building.

Acton Round (12). Two small streams wind round the base of a little wooded hill just off the Bridgnorth–Much Wenlock road. High among the slopes and amid red ploughland and orchards is Acton Round, a few brick cottages, a tiny church and a Queen Anne or William and Mary house. The house itself has long, wide windows and a broad carved cornice below the parapet. The mellow red brick walls have stone dressings and a slate roof with dormers and brick stacks above. This house is clearly the work of an architect and was built as a dower house to Aldenham (the Acton family), and was a farm for a time. The church has a timber-framed belfry and the cruck-framed porch affords a good nesting place for martins. Unfortunately, it has been over-restored, but is worth visiting to see the Stanton monument in the chancel and the little Batty Langley Gothic mortuary chapel, c. 1740–60, opposite the south door. This chapel was designed by T. Pritchard of Shrewsbury, designer of St Julian's, Shrewsbury.

Acton Scott (14). Backed by Ragleth, Hazler and Caer Caradoc Hills in the north and fertile plains to the south, this is a pleasant village and site of a Roman settlement. It was formerly known as Acton Super Montem. The church, with battlemented tower, is mediaeval with very thick walls, but was much restored in the nineteenth century; the Acton chapel is in a pleasant Gothic style of about 1810. There are some good monuments, such as the brass with kneeling figures to Thomas Mytton and family (d. 1577), and the wall monument to Edward Acton, d. 1747, with dark grey marble columns flanking a sarcophagus and rococo shield above. *Acton Hall* is a massive late sixteenth-century Elizabethan brick building with much eighteenth-century work in the interior, set in a superbly laid out park. In 1844, the

remains of a large Roman villa were uncovered here.

Adderley (6). From being a small but busy market town Adderley has shrunk to a mere ghost of its former importance. The church is red sandstone, rebuilt in 1801, and is large and cruciform with a solid classic tower of 1712–13. The pointed windows with their plain crown glass in excellent iron tracery invite and promise an interesting interior. Unfortunately, one is disappointed since the church has been stripped of most of its contemporary fittings and, worst of all, has been sealed off at the crossing. While this may make for convenience it has resulted in half the church being abandoned to dirt and cobwebs, and the more interesting half, too. In this part are hidden the Kilmorey Chapel with its early nineteenth-century armorial glass, a Jacobean screen and monuments to the Corbet and Kilmorey families. The Kilmoreys, Irish peers from nearby Shavington Hall, fought the Corbets of Adderley Park for the use of this chapel. Sir John Corbet, who said "An English baronet is better than an Irish viscount", ordered his Irish footboy to be buried in the Kilmorey chapel over the body of the late Lady Kilmorey. *Shavington Hall*, 1685, might be described as the best house of its period in the county. It is of plain red brick design yet impressive because of its size. The house was altered in 1822 and Norman Shaw took a hand in 1885 with Sir Ernest Newton making further changes in 1903.

Admaston Spa (see Wrockwardine).

Alberbury (7). A border village with good views of the Breidden hills and Rodney's Pillar. An ivy-clad tower is all that remains of the ancient castle. The church is large with a massive thirteenth-century saddle-back tower and an ugly chancel of 1845. This is compensated for by a fine thirteenth-century arcade and nave roof. Old box pews and Jacobean benches remain and there is still a squire's pew. Most of the monuments are to the Leightons of Loton Hall and the Lysters of Rowton Castle. The remains of

Alberbury Priory have been incorporated in a farmhouse and parts of the chapel are still complete. *Loton Park*, now best known for its motor sports, has a red brick Jacobean façade to the south and Queen Anne to the north. *Rowton Castle* is a mainly nineteenth-century romantic revival, castellated and gothicised, on the site of a much earlier castle first burned down by Llewellyn in 1482, rebuilt, and burned again by Commonwealth troops in the seventeenth century. The present building replaces a Queen Anne red brick house and was designed by George Wyatt, 1809–12.

Albrighton by Shifnal (12). A mere stone's throw from its near neighbour Donnington and rapidly becoming a suburb of Wolverhampton. The High Street has lost much of its flavour, but one builder at least has shown some feeling for what is fitting for such a site and his houses settle in very well behind the mature trees that line the street. The red sandstone church is mostly 1853 but there are some good monuments, especially that to Sir John Talbot, d. 1555, in the chancel. The unsightly mess at Cosford is a living reproach to the Ministry of Defence.

Albrighton by Shrewsbury (8). A main road village with some black and white houses. Now utterly ruined by the main road with its constant stream of traffic. The Victorian church is neo-Norman orange-red sandstone with a genuine Norman font and Jacobean pulpit with canopy.

Alveley (15). Off the Kidderminster–Bridgnorth road, looking west towards the Severn above whose bank lies the colliery with unsightly tips spilling down the hill. The church must once have been very fine and the tower is still mainly Norman with eighteenth-century battlements, but Sir Arthur Blomfield was very fierce with the building. There is some beautiful embroidery of about 1500 and an elegant lychgate. Down the road are some good sandstone cottages. *Pool Hall* is eighteenth-century red brick with a two-storied porch and surrounded by a moat. *Coton Hall* is early nineteenth-

Cast-iron tracery at LONGNOR . . .   and ADDERLEY

century stucco with Italianate additions and a tower. "The Nautical William", a large pub on the main road, is white and stark as a battleship, anchored incongruously beside a pretty round house.

Ash (5). A scattered settlement south-west of Whitchurch. The neat and compact nineteenth-century church is separated from the two parts of the village—Ash Magna and Ash Parva—tucked away in a side road. The most remarkable feature of this red brick church is the unusual diagonal buttressing high up on either side of the doorway, creating the impression that it supports the tower. The interior has been restored

during this century. *Ash Hall* is a small eighteenth-century brick house with a hipped roof and large pilasters supporting a pediment. One almost gets the sensation of the rear of the house having been sliced away.

Ashford Bowdler (17). One of the twin Ashfords on either bank of the Teme below Ludlow. A mellow brick and stone village on the west bank of the river, bisected by the railway line to Leominster. Over the level crossing is a charming group of black and white thatched cottages very much in the Herefordshire style. The tiny church on the river bank has a shingled bellcote and a sharp broach spire and Norman

traces in the doors and windows. Otherwise it has been thoroughly "Victorianised" by scraping and inserting cathedral glass but preserving the box pews. The church is almost in the garden of the Georgian *Church House*—white-painted and with an iron porch this is the epitome of the late eighteenth- or early nineteenth-century rectory. *Ashford Hall* is superbly sited on the hill overlooking the village and is glimpsed through the trees of the park. It is a substantial brick house of c. 1760 with a hipped roof and pediment.

Ashford Carbonell (17). A very fine single-arched brick and stone bridge

D

leads into the village, over the Teme. The school is Victorian, with ploughed fields behind, and up a steep lane is the church, surrounded by large yews. The stout tower has a timber-framed belfry with a pyramid cap and Norman south door. Above two slim windows in the east wall is a rare vesica, or almond-shaped, window. The interior has been colour washed. This is a pleasant village, dominated by the Clee Hills in the background, with friendly yet dignified houses. Some are black and white with flowers, others classical with smart white paint and imposing doorways. A good avenue leads to Ashford Court, set amid smooth lawns.

Astley (8). A hamlet in flat country north of Shrewsbury but too close to Shawbury airfield for the enjoyment of rural peace. The church has some Norman fragments but owes most to the nineteenth century. The

forthright epitaph on Rowland Deakin's tombstone (d. 1751, aged 95), begins:

> "Many years I've seen, and
> many things known
> Five Kings, two Queens, an
> usurper on the throne"

Astley House is Grecianised-Georgian yet stands well in its white stucco amid trees.

Astley Abbots (12). A hamlet in the steep lanes near Bridgnorth. The church has a Norman nave and chancel of 1633 but all is much restored and not very exciting. Inside is a good Jacobean pulpit and a Maiden's Garland, hanging in memory of Hannah Phillips who died on the eve of her wedding in 1860. This consists of wooden hoops and several pairs of gloves; the writing is still legible. Beyond the churchyard (where wild strawberries grow) are several pseudo seventeenth-

century houses. Bishop Percy, collector of the "Reliques", was born in Bridgnorth and curate at Astley Abbots 1752–4, later becoming Chaplain to George III, Dean of Carlisle and, finally, Bishop of Dromore.

Aston near Oswestry (4). The Hall is a fine grey stone house of 1780, by Robert Mylne, looking out over a formal garden to the lake beyond and a landscaped park of hardwood trees. There are good iron gates with a coat of arms, opening on to the Oswestry road. All this is private and so is the chapel, once a handsome brick and stone structure of 1742 but elaborately divested of its Georgian character by Street in the '80s.

Aston Botterell (15). Rolling farmland stretches down from the slopes of Brown Clee Hill. The Early English church was refurbished in 1884 and the tower rebuilt, but the

ATCHAM Bridge

interior remains unspoilt and full of interest. There is a good roof to the nave with tie-beams and wind braces, all over dark-varnished pews. A large incised slab commemorates John Botterell, d. 1479, and a six-poster altar tomb bears the recumbent effigies of another John of the same family, d. 1588, together with his wife and kneeling children. In a frame on the S. wall is a document dating from the time of Henry IV. The porch of 1639 leads to a churchyard full of what have been fine tombstones but are now pleasantly decayed.

The *Manor Farm*, former home of the Botterell family, is a stone house incorporating parts of a thirteenth-century hall in the sixteenth-century structure. Across the disused light railway line to Ditton Priors is the peaceful little hamlet of *Bold*, where there is a half-timbered manor house.

Aston Eyre (12). A red brick and half-timber village strung out among orchards near Morville. An unremarkable place but in spring the banks round the church are carpeted with daffodils, alyssum and aubretia in a blaze of colour. The church has been over-restored (though not scraped), but ought to be visited for the sake of the finest piece of Norman sculpture in the county. The twelfth-century tympanum over the south door shows Christ's Entry into Jerusalem with our Lord seated on an elongated ass with enormous ears.

Aston Munslow (see Munslow).

Aston-on-Clun (14). A dependant of Hopesay, a relatively unspoilt stone hamlet with two circular houses and a pretty Gothic inn called the "Kangaroo". The much-pruned poplar in the village is still decorated with flags every Royal Oak Day (29 May), to celebrate the marriage of a Miss Carter, born at Aston House and buried at Sibdon Carwood, and a bequest of hers to the poor of the village. The house, 1820–30, has a handsome Doric porch.

Atcham (11). Apart from the traffic on the main Holyhead road, the

ASTON EYRE

valley of the Severn here is quiet and unspoiled with spacious parkland dotted with clumps of trees. Picturesque and dignified, this area represents the maturity of vision of the landscapists of the end of the eighteenth century. At Atcham itself the Severn is crossed by a modern bridge, but John Gwynne's fine original (1769) remains alongside and at the foot is the red brick "Mytton and Mermaid", once a well-proportioned dower house but now a hotel. Close by is a pretty group of cottages, apricot-washed and with a fanciful Gothic bay and trim gardens. Across the road is the magnificent screen and entrance gates to Attingham Park designed by John Nash. Behind the hotel but still along the Severn bank is the church, red sandstone and a good building spanning the thirteenth to fifteenth centuries. Its dedication is unique— St Eata, a disciple of St Aidan and seventh-century Abbot of Melrose and Lindisfarne. The inside has been scraped and vilely pointed and is very dark. Nevertheless, there are many fine things here, though a

number of them originated elsewhere. The good fifteenth-century glass in the east window in restrained grey, yellow and white came from Bacton in Herefordshire, and there is more from the fifteenth and sixteenth centuries in a north window. The octagonal font is dated 1675 and there is good Flemish and German woodwork in the nave, also ten fine hatchments (Lord Berwick). The incised alabaster slab is a vivid memorial to Edward Burton (d. 1524) and his wife and seven daughters. It was brought here from St Chad's in Shrewsbury (see below). The rectory is red brick Gothic but has been somewhat spoiled. About a mile to the east the R. Tern joins the Severn and Robert Mylne's bridge (1774) forms a more than fitting companion to Gwynne's, with its fine view up to Attingham Hall.

Longner Hall. The present house was built in 1803 to replace a mansion in the "ancient baronial style". It is a very free Tudor composition by John Nash with his partner Humphry Repton to landscape the grounds. In the garden is buried

51

Edward Burton, a Protestant zealot under the Catholic régime of Mary Tudor, who died of joy on hearing the bells of Shrewsbury proclaim the accession of Elizabeth I. The Catholic curate of St Chad's refused to bury him and so his remains were interred in a tomb in his garden.

Cronkhill. A charming white stucco villa in the Italianate style by John Nash, built as a residence for Lord Berwick's agent.

Attingham Park (8). This splendid house was sited by the first Lord Berwick with its finest aspect in line with the Tern bridge on the Shrewsbury road. This is still the best spot from which to view it, with its broad expanse of parkland in front leading to the river and well matured trees forming a backdrop and wings. Humphry Repton planned this in 1797–8 as a fit setting to George Steuart's house, and his Red Book outlining his scheme is still kept there. Noel Hill (later the first Lord Berwick) wanted a grandiose design and in 1785 Steuart provided him with a fine, yet simple, house in Grinshill stone enriched with a massive portico with a pediment carried on four tall columns, and wings on either side. The property is now owned by the National Trust and is leased to the Shropshire County Council as an Adult College. It is possible to view part of the superb interior with its plaster ceilings and John Nash's picture gallery (1805), with its iron-framed roof cast at Coalbrookdale. Attingham is the one remaining house by Steuart in the county.

Badger (12). Approaching from Albrighton the road dives through a tunnel, over which runs the tree-lined carriage drive of the now-demolished Badger Hall. Cottages nestle together round the brick-walled garden of the former Hall and the road climbs up towards the church. Here a surprise awaits the visitor, for round the corner one comes upon a pool on the edge of which is the church. This is the top-most of a descending chain of ponds, part of the landscaping of the Badger estate; a little classical temple,

◁ ATTINGHAM PARK

▽ Longner Hall, ATCHAM

probably by one of the Wyatts, also remains. Heavily restored in 1834 and later, the church is rich in nineteenth-century monuments by Flaxman, Chantrey and John Gibson and will prove of great interest to those who enjoy their work. The font is a well-designed classical marble copy of that in St Bride's, Fleet Street. In the E. window are some fragments of early glass.

Barrow (12). A little handful of houses and a church resting high on the edge of Willey Park, a couple of miles outside Much Wenlock. A row of plain brick almshouses, backs to the road, was built in 1816, though founded on another site in 1612. The church is probably one of the oldest and certainly one of the most interesting, historically, in the county. The chancel is Saxon and Dean Cranage believed it to date from the eighth century. The nave is early Norman and has three deeply splayed windows. The W. doorway to the tower, and original entrance to the church, has a tall unmoulded arch and tympanum with almost unique decoration of lozenges and saltire crosses—not enhanced by the clumsy insertion of electric cables. The squat stone tower is late Norman, built in four stages with brick battlements and a pyramidal roof added in the eighteenth century. A classical brick and stone S. porch was added in 1705. The interior was well restored by Street in 1852 but in 1895 the plaster and mural paintings were stripped from the walls and cathedral glass made to darken the church. It has lost all its texture and architectural interest and is now no more than an album for the antiquarian. There is a fine cast-iron monument in the church-yard, 1807.

Baschurch (8). Was a settlement of some importance in Saxon times but had already declined by the twelfth century. It now straggles along the main road with an ugly rash of bungalows. The older part of the village forms a compact group round the church and inn with a few black-and-white buildings. The well-kept red sandstone church has been much renewed but the fine tower is unspoiled. Thomas Telford

was responsible for major works here in 1790 and his account for £1,230 still hangs in the church.

The Laurels is a good timber-framed house with brick infilling. Dame Agnes Hunt opened her hospital at *Boratton Park* near here (now a school), and later founded the Park Hall Orthopaedic Hospital at Oswestry.

Batchcott (see Richard's Castle).

Battlefield (8). Beyond the northern fringe of Shrewsbury one emerges into green fields, the site of the Battle of Shrewsbury, 1403, when Henry IV beat, and slew, Harry Hotspur. It is very peaceful now with nothing but a large church and a late-Victorian red brick vicarage. Henry IV founded the church as a thanksgiving for victory and a statue of him in armour still remains in a niche at the E. end, well-weathered yet recognisable. S. Pountney Smith was responsible for the openwork parapets and pinnacles and, though one fears the worst as a result, when one enters the church it is both a surprise and a relief to find it relatively unspoiled. Sufficient remains to allow one to imagine the church as it must have been in all its glory. The interior is splendidly light and spacious with only the screen dividing nave from chancel. An intimation of the original splendour of the glass can be gleaned from the fragments remaining in the vestry windows.

Baystonhill (11). This parish was formed in the mid-nineteenth century from parts of the parishes of Condover and St Julian's, Shrewsbury, and a new church, 1843, by E. Haycock was built close to the now neglected village green. The slim, stepped tower is curious but the remainder of the village is nothing but a sprawl of mediocre dormitory housing for Shrewsbury. The seventeenth-century manor house is still in Condover parish, and Bomere Pool, close by, set among trees, is the largest of the lakes mentioned under Betton Strange. Mary Webb lived at Lyth Hill for a while and this pool is the San Mere of *Precious Bane*; the novel is set in this district, *not* Ellesmere. *Lythwood Hall*, built

c. 1782 by George Steuart for a Mr Blakeway with lottery prize money, is altered beyond recognition.

Beckbury (12). A knot of red brick houses and cottages cluster about the church and Hall but council houses sprawl away to destroy much of the village's character. A fine background of yews sets off the pinky-grey sandstone church which is mainly nineteenth century, apart from a neat Georgian tower with pyramid roof. The interior is much restored but it has a pleasant air, light and cool on a summer's day. The proportions are unusual: this church must be at least as broad as it is long. There is a delicately incised monumental slab to Richard Houghton (d. 1505) and his wife, with their ten elegantly clad children at their feet. In the upper part of the village is an unusually good nineteenth-century school house.

Bedstone (13). On a hillside, between two streams, looking across to the prehistoric camp of Castle Ditches to the west. A thatched cottage and curious Victorian school house with a patterned tile roof nestle near the church. The door opens directly into the nave of this Norman building with its charming windows, some of them original. The simple chancel arch reveals a triple window at the E. end. The nineteenth-century restorers worked with more than usual sensitivity here. *Manor Farm* is an H-shaped timber-framed house with a stone front dated 1775 but with two huge crucks of the former hall behind. *Bedstone Court* (now a school) is a large, ostentatious pseudo black-and-white mansion of 1884.

Benthall (12). A remote and unexpected spot near Broseley approached by a tree-lined road. The church of 1667 replaces the old one burnt down in the Civil War. It is small, charming and singularly well restored; white paint contrasts well with the dark box pews and little gallery. Clear glass lets in plenty of light. The surprising additions of 1893 (porch and staircase approach to the gallery) might well have won a *Studio* competition at the time. The

Hall (N.T.) is a superb grey stone building of c. 1583 with a rich garden and a long low front of mullioned windows looking out over pastoral country. The little drawing-room with its white-painted panelling is wholly delightful. *Benthall Edge*, accessible only on foot, is a tree-covered slope dropping almost sheer into the Ironbridge Gorge. The tradition of clay-working is perpetuated by a pipe works; at one time a highly glazed earthenware was made at Benthall.

Berrington (11). The large, weather-worn pink sandstone tower of the church dominates a district of small green hills. Cobbles front the mellow red brick cottages and the approach to the church itself. The interior has been scraped and Evans' E. window and the placing of the organ make the chancel impossibly dark. However, there is a Norman font with very primitive carvings of masks in relief and a late thirteenth-century oak effigy of a knight in a recess in the S. wall, very much like the one at Pitchford, but not as good. Beyond the jumbled table-tombs outside the S. porch (one has a very delicately engraved plate of 1796) is the black and white gabled *Manor House* with a stone roof, dated 1658 on the door.

Berwick (8). A mere two miles from the centre of Shrewsbury yet utterly quiet and peaceful. A pair of handsome Greek stone lodges frame the entrance to the drive up to Berwick House, built in 1731 by Francis Smith for the Powys family. This fine red brick and stone house looks out over a garden stepped down in terraces to the Severn below with a splendid backcloth of woods beyond. Remodelling in the Italianate manner has disturbed the original concept yet not wholly destroyed it. In the park is a group of almshouses (1672) grouped round a courtyard and entered though a stone archway. These were built by Sir Samuel Jones, who was also responsible for the chapel close by. The tower was added when the house was built and the chancel at the end of the nineteenth century. The interior is white paint and oak panelling with the original eighteenth-century box

pews and wrought-iron communion rails. The panelled barrel-vault is in keeping and the inside has more coherence than the outside. The blocked S. porch has a fireplace, a reminder of the time when it served as a family pew. Berwick House is the home of the oldest Jersey herd in England.

Betton Strange (11) and Betton Alkmere consist of two houses and a church of 1858 (at Betton Strange) down a lane which is a dead end. The church is within the "boundary walk" of Betton Hall. The green country between here and Baystonhill embraces a series of unexpected woodland lakes and pools: Betton Pool and Bomere Pool.

Bettws-y-Crwyn (13). "The prayer house of the skins" (fleeces). On a windswept hilltop, about 1,400 feet up, this is one of the highest villages in Shropshire, with views over much of the south of the county and the desolate hills of Radnor. This is sheep country and has given rise to the local Clun and Kerry breeds. The church lies back behind a screen of conifers with raspberries growing wild by the gate. The Victorians were heavy handed here but left the splendid fifteenth-century roof alone and fortunately did not disturb the delicate, open Perp. screen. There is a double-decker Jacobean pulpit and font-cover and rough benches with crude poppy-head ends. The farm names are still painted on the bench-ends in blue and some very good eighteenth-century slate tablets by local craftsmen remain.

Bicton (8). A decayed village off the Holyhead road near Shrewsbury. A white stuccoed manor house, a ruined and overgrown eighteenth-century church, a red brick Georgian farm with a monkey puzzle and a duckpond make up what there is. The new church (1866) has a very ugly tower. To the north the Severn makes a spectacular meander, known as the Isle, in which are the remains of a moated castle.

Billingsley (15). The church was almost entirely rebuilt, and spoiled, in 1875, so that little of any interest remains. The paintings on the south

wall were destroyed in the name of "restoration" but some pictures remain to show what the church once looked like. An ugly Frenchi-fied bell-cote now crowns the nave but the good timber porch with carved barge-boards survives. The church is set on a ridge in the Wheatland country, rich, swooping fields and orchards between Bridg-north and Bewdley. Dr Thomas Hyde (born here in 1636) was principal of the Bodleian Library and the first Englishman to master Chinese.

Bishop's Castle (13). Irregular streets climb up a hill in this small market town on the edge of the Clun Forest. The church at the bottom of the hill has a squat unbuttressed Norman tower which is dwarfed by the Victorian nave. A varied collection of architectural styles, from Georgian to modern, in grey stone, brick and half-timber stand cheek by jowl in streets which remind one of some of the inland Welsh towns. The curious brick and stone school dated 1875 stands close to a large and imposing Midland Bank—basically eighteenth century but with Carolean and Italianate additions all crisply painted in grey and white. Clay pipes are still for sale in the barber's shop. At the top of the hill the climax of the street is the *Town Hall*, brick and stone, about 1765, with two circular windows to the basement, which was the lock-up. On the left of the Town Hall is a steep, narrow, cobbled passage, above which is the so-called *House on Crutches*, its upper storey supported by two wooden posts. This passage leads to the Market Place, but the Old Market Hall, 1775, has recently been demolished. No remains above ground of the Castle, but the Castle Hotel bowling green is on the site of the keep.

Bishop's Castle (formerly the smallest borough in England) was a rotten borough and prior to 1832 returned two Members to Parliament. In 1820 four candidates each polled 87 votes, and since no provision had been made for a casting vote they were all elected. There was formerly a mug in Ludlow Museum commemorating the disenfranchisement of Bishop's Castle.

The history of the Bishop's Castle

Railway, which connected the town with Craven Arms 10½ miles away, is a pathetic one. The line was begun in 1863 but opposition postponed its opening until 1866. Then the Company went bankrupt as the money ran out and the bankruptcy was still not discharged when the line closed in 1935, when the rails were taken up and the rolling stock sold. It suffered endless trials. At one time a fence was put across the line and two men set to guard it by the executors of a landowner who had not been paid. On another occasion the line was flooded, a train abandoned by its engine and a bridge washed away. The line was one of the prettiest in the country, following the course of the road and river up the Onny Gorge. The former stations at Stetford Bridge, Horderley, Plowden and Lydham Heath are all in a decrepit state.

Bitterley (15). A higgledy-piggledy village on the slopes of Titterstone Clee with a small brook idling through it. Orchards and green meadows and glowing red soil in the winter fields. The church stands apart from the village and close by Bitterley Court, a part Jacobean house with a late Georgian façade, set in a pleasant park. A huge squat tower capped by a shingled turret and broach spire dominates the Norman church and houses some good bells. In spring the churchyard is a blaze of colour from the many flowering trees and shrubs. Unfortunately, the Victorian restorations have given the interior an impersonal museum-like atmosphere, yet the many monuments to the Powys, Walcot and other families record centuries of history and service. Particularly fine is the kneeling figure of Timothy Lucy, in armour and puffed breeches, who died in 1616. *Henley Hall* on the Kidderminster road is an impressively large red brick house of mixed styles and history. The early Georgian wrought-iron gates are especially good. John Newborough, a former headmaster of Eton, founded a school in Bitterley in 1712.

◁ Telford's St. Mary Magdalene, BRIDGNORTH

Great Bolas (9). Flat meadows slide down to the banks of the peaceful R. Tern. The church is of mellow red brick of 1729, with a tall and massive tower capped with a parapet and well-shaped urns instead of the usual pinnacles; it was designed by John Willdigg. The interior is wholly delightful with seventeenth-century box pews and plastered and white-painted walls and ceiling. Clear-glazed semi-circular windows in the seventeenth-century chancel are seen through a similarly shaped chancel arch with freshly painted Royal Arms above, and in front stands the eighteenth-century pulpit with its high sounding-board. A little gallery is tucked in under the W. tower. In the late eighteenth century the Earl of Burleigh lived here, incognito, for a time, and married a local beauty, the miller's daughter, Sarah Hoggins. They lived in Burleigh (Bolas) Villa, a neat little Georgian house, until he succeeded to the family estates in Lincolnshire on the death of the ninth Earl of Exeter. Tennyson's poem relates the story of their courtship and marriage, though with much poetic licence.

Boningale (12). Near Albrighton. There are several good black-and-white houses here, especially Church Farm, close by the little church. Its roof is of unusually low pitch but the interior has been rather harshly treated.

Boraston (17). Lies on the S. slopes of Brown Clee Hill in a remote situation, reached by winding lanes. This is an attractive spot with red brick Georgian houses and tiny cottages with gay gardens and well-clipped hedges. The church has a plain Norman doorway and low-raftered roof but owes most of its structure to the Victorian restoration of 1887. The font, with spiral fluting on the bowl, came from Buildwas.

Boscobel (12). Enjoys an especially favoured place in the legends surrounding Charles II and his flight after the miserable failure of his supporters at the Battle of Worcester in 1651. It was here that Charles fled, staying first at White Ladies and Spring Coppice, after which he "got up into a great oak, that had been lopt some three or four years before, and being grown out again, very bushy and thick, could not be seen through, and here we staid all the day. . . . while we were in this tree we see soldiers going up and down, in the thicket of the wood, searching for persons escaped, we seeing them, now and then, peeping out of the wood." (Charles's own account.) The following night was spent in hiding in Boscobel House itself whence the King set out for Bristol. The house is Jacobean, 1630, and owes its fame entirely to its history; the Royal Oak is, sadly, almost certainly not the original but an offspring, yet Royal Oak Day is still

The Severn at BRIDGNORTH

celebrated on 29 May (the day Charles was restored to the throne). See also Aston-on-Clun. For a highly romantic account of King Charles's adventures one should read Harrison Ainsworth's *Boscobel*; for a strictly factual account there is an excellent Guide published by the Ministry of Public Building and Works, in whose charge Boscobel House and White Ladies Priory now remain. White Ladies House has vanished and all that now remains of the Augustinian nunnery are the old ruins of the twelfth-century church.

Bouldon (14). A cluster of farm buildings surround the delightful little corrugated-iron parish church in its pale blue-grey and white paint nestling under the northern slopes of Brown Clee Hill.

Bourton (11). A mainly stone-built village in Corvedale where a little road leads down from a crossing point on Wenlock Edge. Farms cluster round on higher ground and the post office is reached by a little bridge over a rippling stream. Further up the hill is Bourton Manor with the Norman church below. With yew trees round about and the familiar weather-boarded belfry with pyramid cap there is some evidence of nineteenth-century renewal. Fortunately, the character of this church has not been destroyed and a tall Norman doorway leads into a very pleasant interior with fanciful ends to the box pews and a tiny chancel *and* gallery. The carving on the pulpit is superbly rich and it stands supported on a single column. *Bourton Manor* is a rambling country house by Norman Shaw, 1870, incorporating parts of an earlier building. It has two half-timbered gables and a tile hung first-floor, all over a massive stone-arched doorway. Sixteen chimneys make a startling and rich roof-line to this picturesque place.

Bridgnorth (12). A town dramatically (and strategically) placed on high ground overlooking the River Severn. No map can prepare one for the impact of this town as one approaches on the Kidderminster or Wellington roads; the buildings cling to the cliff-face and are surmounted by the main town marching on the sky-line

and led from either end by the two churches. Narrow lanes and endless flights of steps wind up from the river bank to the main street, but the most exciting route is by the cliff railway—2½p return and a gradient of 1:1⅓! On the way you may pass Bishop Percy's House, a beautifully preserved black and white building of 1580 and former home of the eighteenth-century antiquary and poet who collected the ballads known as "Percy's Reliques". (See Astley Abbots.) St Leonard's church closes the view at the top of narrow Church Street which opens unexpectedly into the Close. The church is now surrounded by closely-mown lawns and the whole encircled and enclosed by an assortment of almshouses, cottages, eighteenth-century brick and even a small factory. The result is a cross between a village green and a cathedral close and creates a very real sense of *place*. The "very fayre" church (Leland) was almost completely destroyed during the Civil War when it was garrisoned by Royalist troops. Having been driven from the castle they made the church their ammunition store, and the Parliamentarians, turning the cannons on the church, scored a direct hit from the castle. The ensuing fire destroyed most of the High Town and thus much of the rebuilding dates from that Easter Tuesday in 1646. Richard Baxter was curate and lived in a cottage close by the church. The castle was dismantled and the former Governor's house taken as the main building on which a new (East Castle) street was laid out with Thomas Telford's St Mary Magdalene as the focal point at the castle end. From there it is possible to walk back into the town centre along the cliff walk with its superb views up the valley to the beginning of the Ironbridge Gorge. Passing the cast-iron fronted Waterloo House (1802), and with a lovely Weslyan chapel in blue brick and grey and lilac paint round the corner, one comes again into the wide High Street. The Town Hall straddles the road, echoing the town gate further on, and is matched in interest by the many fine inns on either side. The Swan is splendid in black and white and incorporates an open-fronted shop which can

surely have changed little since the seventeenth century. The ground falls away steeply again to the S.W. where both old and new roads wind tortuously back down to Low Town. A splendid iron footbridge leaps across the ravine to the former railway station, no longer in regular use but now the home of the Severn Valley Railway Company. This body of enthusiasts maintain and run preserved locomotives here, and there are plans to reopen the line to Bewdley to tourist traffic. The line must surely be one of the most beautiful in the country, following as it does the valley of the Severn. It is most appropriate that Bridgnorth should be the centre of such activity, for it was here at Raistrick's foundry in Low Town that the first railway locomotive was built for Trevithick in 1804 and also the Catch-Me-Who-Can which ran in the famous Euston trials a few years later. Like so many towns, Bridgnorth does not give up all its secrets very readily, but there is a wealth of drama, visual and historic, in the quiet town so popular with week-end visitors.

Brockton (11). A mere handful of houses at a crossroads in Corvedale. A mound marks the site of a motte and bailey castle.

Bromfield (14). Ludlow Racecourse lies beside the now derelict conifer-shaded railway station, with its red brick and white ironwork grandstand. The graceful old stone bridge is now superseded where the new road sweeps away to avoid the village, leaving the church intact on its wooded promontory between the Onny and the Teme. The sadly neglected half-timbered gatehouse was once the entrance to a twelfth-century Benedictine Priory. After the Dissolution the fine Norman chancel arch was sealed off and the present chancel formed part of the private dwelling of one Charles Foxe and remained as such until 1658 when it was restored to divine service. The present chancel ceiling is covered by a superbly vulgar painting in greys, blues and white by Thomas Francis, 1672. This

BROMFIELD ceiling ▷

58

BUILDWAS Abbey

surprising piece of folk art has been described as "the best example of the worst style of ecclesiastical art". Of the rest of the church, entered by a porch of a size fit for a cathedral, it must be said that Bodley's restoration (1890) did not disturb the strong, broad proportions and much remains from the thirteenth century and fourteenth century including the N. arcade. The rich interior has been scraped and there is a deal too much greenish cathedral glass which accords ill with the pink sandstone. One of the roof beams bears the inscription "The Rufe was made by me, John Geth 1577", and parts of an Elizabethan screen are along the W. wall. Henry Hill Hickman, 1800–30, "the earliest known pioneer of anaesthesia by inhalation", is commemorated by a centenary tablet. An avenue of forty Irish yews still marks the approach to the E. end of the church.

Oakley Park, eighteenth-century brick, overlooks the Teme where a broad shallow waterfall foams into a sweep beside Gothic cottages.

Brompton and Rhiston (10). Two remote, churchless hamlets on the Montgomeryshire border—almost Wales, and in a lovely Welsh near-mountain landscape.

Broseley (12). A decayed manufacturing town of great beauty, textural and forlorn. In the eighteenth century Broseley was in the heart of Britain's coal and iron belt and the only urban centre in the Coalbrookdale coalfield as evidenced by the remaining street names such as Foundry Lane and Foundry Court. John Wilkinson (an ironmaster of equal standing with the better-known Abraham Darby) had his works here. He was a great enthusiast for cast iron and left instructions in his will that he be buried in an iron coffin. In 1776 he installed the first Boulton and Watt steam engine to be sold from the

60

Soho Works and was responsible for the first iron barge, 1787. The large church, in Perpendicular style, was built in 1845 when the town was still prosperous. Solid tower with battlements, nave with clerestory, cast-iron gates to churchyard and several massively elaborate cast-iron tombstones. Church Street contains some of the best houses including The Lawns, 1727, home of John Wilkinson, with large eighteenth-century bow windows but in a sorry state now. There are still manufacturers in Broseley: of drainage pipes and roofing tiles. The local clay is particularly suitable for making pipes and this is an industry of long standing. The Legg family made the first pipes here and were succeeded by the Rodens. Noah Roden, 1770–1829, brought churchwardens and straws to perfection and supplied most of the London clubs and coffee houses of the day. George Forester of Willey Park (near Broseley), bought a box of Roden's pipes and sent them to Roden as the perfect article to imitate. Rev. Charles Hartshorne, antiquary and author of topographical works on Shropshire, Northumberland and Northamptonshire, was born at Broseley in 1803.

Bucknell (16). A pretty village, almost on the county boundary, in the gentler part of the Clun valley, with hill slopes towering to the west. Local tradition gives Bucknell as the site of the last battle between Caractacus and the Roman invaders, as described by Tacitus. Certainly, at Coxall Knoll nearby there are remains of a British camp. Some thatch, stone and half-timber houses and a restored Norman church with an early Norman front and huge yew trees surrounding it. On the church tower is an unusual blue vitreous enamel clock face. A Baptist chapel, 1871, and a derelict Methodist chapel with good lettering on a sandstone plaque of 1849. Bucknell station is a neat Gothic building of 1860 with barge-boards, Tudor-style chimneys and freestone walls.

Buildwas (12). The great ox-bow sweeps of the Severn change abruptly as the river begins to enter the gorge towards Ironbridge. The best

BUILDWAS: The power station

approaches are down the steep, winding road through the woods from Much Wenlock, a glorious blaze of colour in autumn, or along the valley itself from Leighton with the road tucked on a ledge above the flood-plain. Where this countryside was once punctuated by smoking foundry chimneys downstream now loom the massive cooling towers of the two power stations. Seen from afar, these towers do not disturb the landscape, but the untidy clutter round their bases and the striding pylons far outweigh their charm. Buildwas Abbey, founded at the river crossing by Roger de Clinton, dates from about 1150, and in spite of the meticulous mowing and tidying by the M.P.B.W. still preserves some of its simple majesty. The picturesque decay, so beloved by eighteenth- and nineteenth-century engravers, is arrested, yet on a winter afternoon, with a low sun, one can recapture a little of their vision. Much of the Grinshill stone was carried away to build the little church in 1720 (cast-iron plate in the porch), but nineteenth-century gothicising has spoilt the classic mood. The W. gallery is now the best feature. Close by is a charming Victorian school with gleaming white barge-boards and black-and-white school house beside. An ugly County Council bridge incorporates a fragment of what was Telford's first iron bridge, an historic step forward from Darby's masterpiece two miles downstream.

Burford (17). A small village standing in meadows beside the Teme where Herefordshire, Worcestershire and Shropshire meet. Tenbury Wells (Worcs.) is a near neighbour across the river. A woody lane leads to the rectory and Burford House, a red brick Georgian house of 1728, well sited with the woods on the hill behind, across the river. The charming gardens which surround the house were only recently established yet look remarkably mature: they are open to the public during the summer months. The church stands close by and, though old, is mostly attributable to Sir Aston Webb (1889). The tower is handsome, and largely new in its outward appearance, but it is for the monuments

that this church is most memorable. The best are to the Cornwall family and range from a fourteenth-century brass to Elizabeth de Cornewayle to an alabaster figure of Princess Elizabeth, daughter of John of Gaunt and wife of Sir John Cornewayle. The most impressive is the large, painted triptych on the N. wall of the chancel, fully eleven feet high. On the outside of the wings are figures of the Apostles, while on the inside is a painting of Richard Cornwall (d. 1568) with his father and mother. None of these (nor the other monuments) are of exceptional quality but they do contribute greatly to the richness of the interior. There are some affinities with Tong, but that church far surpasses Burford in variety of interest and contrasts of texture. It is, nevertheless, worth seeing.

Burlton (see Loppington).

Burwarton (14). A stately village on the Ludlow–Bridgnorth road with the magnificent park of the Hall stretching up over the wooded E. slopes of Brown Clee Hill and Abdon Burf. Burwarton Hall is an Italianate house by A. Salvin but has been partly demolished and the remainder renovated. Across the road from its pink-washed lodge is a rhododendron-lined path leading to the church, also by Salvin, 1877, of a rather harsh design, in rock-faced yellow stone.

The ivied ruins of the old Norman church still stand across the brook from the new building, which is now closed. The Boyne Arms is a remarkably good Georgian stone inn tucked in a corner near the church.

Calverhall (or **Cloverley** or **Corra**) (5). A hamlet in undulating country scattered with small ponds, between Whitchurch and Market Drayton. W. Eden Nesfield was responsible for much of the building here. His *Cloverley Hall* was built in 1862 in an Elizabethan red brick manner and was a pioneer of domestic architecture. Little remains now to reveal the ingenious internal plan, merely the connecting ranges and outbuildings. Nesfield was at work here again in 1878 when he renewed

and extended the church, principally by knocking down one end of the almshouses (1724), and joining on his new south aisle. The interior is not especially interesting but there is a good window by Morris and Burne-Jones (c. 1875) in the chancel. The "Jack of Corra" was a leather bottle, kept in this parish, from which any traveller could drink beer for a penny.

Cardeston (8) church has a nave and chancel of 1748 and Victorian tower, a poor wall painting and ghastly green-painted pews. A little Gothic organ lies unused in a corner. In the tower is a photograph of a print of Lady Leighton's celebrated miniature of the "Ladies of Llangollen" (Lady Eleaner Butler and Miss Sarah Ponsonby). This engraving enjoyed considerable contemporary popularity and prints fetched enormous sums. Lady Leighton donated £500 from the proceeds to Cardeston church for the rebuilding of the tower.

Wattlesborough Hall. About three miles W. of Cardeston. A Georgian farmhouse which has among its farm buildings the square keep of a Norman castle, one of the Border chain between Caus and Alberbury.

Cardington (11). Best approached by a narrow, winding road from All Stretton, under the gaunt ridge of Caer Caradoc, passing black-and-white houses and farms. The village is among the gentler grassy hills, built of large stones, and is just like a Devon moorland village. The church tower, recently plastered, takes a pinkish hue from the local sand and this, together with the mushroom and gilt of the clock face, makes a beautiful contrast with the cool grey stone of the nave. Inside, the structure has been much renewed, but there are subtle harmonies and contrasts to be found among the pale old timbers of the nave and the dark beams and braces of the chancel. The walls are washed in pale grey with tablets in slate, marble, copper and brass and a mid-seventeenth-century painted memorial. A good monument to Chief Justice Leighton, d. 1607, is in the chancel with his family kneeling in front of the tomb-chest. The handsome timber porch is dated 1639. Leighton lived at *Plaish Hall*, the earliest house of any substance to be built in brick in this county. It dates mainly from about 1540, on an H-plan, with stone quoins and blue brick to enrich the surfaces. Above are three fine moulded chimneys in the ornate style of the period. *Chatwall Hall* is a lonely and isolated stone and timber seventeenth-century house, a former home of the Corfields. *Chatwall Farm* is a Queen Anne stone building with gables similar to those at the Hall. Near Cardington is Hoar Edge, where the sandstone was quarried for use as stone-slates for roofing, as can still be seen at Much Wenlock.

Caynham (17). There are fine views of the Clee hills to be seen from this village set amid farms and orchards. The church, approached along a yew-arched pathway, is dismally dark even on a sunny afternoon. Although some Norman fragments remain, the church was almost entirely rebuilt by James Brooks in 1885 and, in spite of the unusual triple arch to the chancel and its vaulting, the result is cold and lifeless.

Chapel Lawn (13). An unspoiled Victorian stone village in the mountainous district near Clun and under the wooded slopes of Hodre Hill. The stone church by E. Haycock, 1844, is dull and hard.

Chelmarsh (15) (see also Eardington). A ridge village with an imposing brick and stone eighteenth-century church tower. The grey stone church has a fine row of Decorated windows along the S. wall. High on the E. wall is the reputed burial place of a monk's heart. Views can be glimpsed of the marina developing on a reservoir belonging to the S. Staffs. Water Board. A rare tower clock in the church, probably the oldest in the county.

Cheney Longville (see Wistanstow).

Cherrington (see Tibberton).

Cheswardine (6). A village set on a hill with good views over flat country. Of the church, the Perp. west tower and the very fine E.E.

chancel chapel are original, the rest being in a good E.E. style by J. L. Pearson, 1888–9. There are royal arms of Charles II, also Georgian (carved), and several good windows by Kempe, 1892–9. Two old brasses in the floor of the nave are dated 1610 and 1632. Outside, on the tower walls are carvings of a Staffordshire knot and a Talbot dog, and on the buttresses a lion and dragon. *Cheswardine Hall* is red brick neo-Elizabethan with a Tuscan porch, 1875.

Chetton (14). A remote and lovely village high on a spur of Brown Clee and up a dead-end off the Bridgnorth-Ludlow road. The church has been rebuilt several times and only the S. door and chancel are mediaeval. The arch-moulding rests on two large heads, very naïve in their carving and obviously the work of a secular mason. The tombstones here are good and a path leads from the churchyard to an old inn with pleasant views from its garden. A modern "Georgian style" rectory disrupts the harmony of the scene.

Chetwynd (9). On the busy main road, north of Newport, but, in spite of its situation, the setting is pleasantly rural. Conifers and oaks, and a lake in the large park surrounding the gabled seventeenth-century Chetwynd House which lies in a hollow and is screened from the road. Close by stand a large brick stable block and dovecote.

The church is one of the best examples of Victorian building we have seen in Shropshire. It was designed by Benjamin Ferrey, 1865–7, in rock-faced red sandstone with a tower capped by an elegant and well-proportioned broach spire. Large marble columns with richly carved capitals separate the spacious nave from the chancel. The detail is in complete harmony with the impressive interior.

Child's Ercall (9). A not very inspiring village standing on slightly higher ground than the surrounding heath. Many of the houses are of hard red Midland brick. The church is pleasantly well weathered with a good Perp. tower. Victorian chancel. Inside, the pink sandstone of the

nave is beautifully set off by cream-painted plaster and the whole church was full of the scent of carnations. A hagioscope and a very fine brass memorial plate.

Chirbury (10) stands at the junction of six roads, looking west to the Berwyn Mountains and backed by Corndon and Stapley Hill. This is a charming mellow brick, stone and half-timber village in a relatively unknown and unspoilt corner of the county. The church is very large, the nave being formerly part of a thirteenth-century priory (chancel 1733), with a massive tower. There are a number of good tombstones in the churchyard, near the tower, with some unusually fine examples of nineteenth-century letter-cutting. Inside the whitewashed tower are some hatchments and a good eighteenth-century memorial to members of the Prichard family. Blomfield was rather heavy-handed in his restoration but the overall feeling is pleasant. A unique matrix for casting tokens of the Virgin and Child, for sale to pilgrims, was dug up in the churchyard here. There is a black-and-white *school* (1675) near the *vicarage*, which formerly housed a library of some 164 chained books left to the village by Lord Herbert of Chirbury, poet, wit and ambassador to Paris, born at Eyton in 1583. He was the elder brother of the better known poet George Herbert. The books are now in the County Archives at Shrewsbury. *Marrington Hall*, on the Ludlow road, built in 1595, is a well restored black and white house resembling Pitchford.

Chirk (4) (Denbighshire). From the road bridge beside the pub, a genuine "Last in England", a view of Telford's spectacular aqueduct for the Ellesmere Canal Company (1796–1801). Behind and above it with the same number of arches is the railway viaduct.

Church Aston (9). A southern suburb of Newport. The red sandstone church with white stone dressings is by Street, 1867. It is light and bright but lacking in character. There is a lead (flèche) spire above the nave.

Church Preen (11). Approached along a maze of high-banked winding lanes, this hamlet is almost hidden among the hill slopes. Even more inconspicuous amidst the towering trees is the creeper-clad church just beyond an open space with a pond and cedar-boarded Forestry Commission houses. Close by the church is the *Manor House*, standing on the site of the old priory and incorporating parts of an older building. It was designed by Norman Shaw, 1870–2, though all but the ground floor has now been demolished. Across a courtyard is the thirteenth-century monastic church of unusual proportions. It is only 13 feet wide but 70 feet long, the nave and chancel being all in one. The interior, white-painted and well lit by electricity, is very attractive with its Jacobean pulpit and reading desk. A tiny south chapel was added, c. 1920–5, very skilfully done and battlemented to be in keeping with the Manor House. Outside is a massive iron-bound yew and ancient beech, and a few steps away one is carried straight into the mood of the Picturesque with little stone-arched bridges, waterfalls and laurels. Quite delightful and unexpected. At the crossroads is the village *school*, also by Norman Shaw, a handsome L-shaped design with a large timber-framed gable and dormer windows.

Church Pulverbatch (11). This is hilly country S.W. of Shrewsbury with lovely views. A picture of the church in 1653 shows it with small windows and a little bellcote, but the present sandstone tower dates from 1773 with a blocked doorway with Gibbs surround and a flight of steps up to a door in the tower. A window and door lead through to a gallery inside the church. The nave and chancel are mid-nineteenth century although the box pews and pulpit are contemporary with the tower and look a little out of place—too good for the rest, really. Down the hill a good Georgian brick farm is rotting away and its once-pretty arcade of yew hedge is smothering it. There was once a castle here—the motte remains.

◁ CLAVERLEY Church and Rectory

Church Stretton (11). For the author, childhood memories of visits to Church Stretton and "Little Switzerland" must colour his whole view of Shropshire. This *was* the county and perhaps it was no bad place to discover first, with picnics and teas in Carding Mill Valley. The Official Handbook of The Church Stretton Advancement Association (1912) gives a clear picture of the development of the town and its nature: "Church Stretton is the centre of the Hill District of South Shropshire. It lies in an open valley between the Longmynd and Caradoc ranges, and is 13 miles south of Shrewsbury, on the main line from Bristol and South Wales to Manchester and the north. . . . Church Stretton itself consists of the original High Street, . . . on the Longmynd side of the valley and the old Roman Road, Watling Street, nearly parallel with it on the Caradoc side. Crossing these is the Sandford Avenue leading eastwards to the village of Hope Bowdler. . . . Thirty to forty years ago Church Stretton was a small market town, living very much its own life and little disturbed by outside influences. During the summer some few families would come in order to enjoy the hills and invigorating air, and picnic parties . . . might frequently be seen in the Carding Mill Valley." Of the virtues of the town it was said: "Not only has the climate a generally tonic and invigorating effect, but it also has the valuable quality of excercising a somewhat tranquillising influence on the nervous system and circulation. . . . It affords a fine rest cure for those who have more or less succumbed to the effects of the general rush and ever present high pressure of our twentieth-century civilisation." This last probably refers to the advent of the motor car in the town, but contemporary photographs reveal nothing more dangerous than a pony and trap! Nevertheless, although the popularity of Church Stretton as a health resort may have waned, the sudden upsurge of building in the '80s and '90s has given the place a marked Victorian flavour that is changing only slowly. As its development was so late, there are not a great many buildings of beauty in the town, but its character is consistent, and its features include half-timber, yuccas, firs, ragged planning, cleanliness, rusticated stone and tennis courts. The surrounding hills are Church Stretton's glory and fully justify their fame and popularity. Hazler, Caer Caradoc and Lawley on the one hand with their splendid outlines, and on the other, the climb up into Carding Mill Valley with its splendid scenery of bracken-covered slopes and waterfall or, by taking the upper road, the tortuous ascent to the Longmynd. From the top one looks out across the batches and cwms to Caradoc, and beyond, in the distance, the Wrekin and the plain of the Severn round Shrewsbury. Behind stretches ten miles of moorland with the Stiperstones and the Long Mountain beyond. There are three Strettons in the valley— Church Stretton in the centre, All Stretton 1½ miles to the north and Little Stretton the same distance to the south. At *All Stretton* is the Manor House and Old Hall, while *Little Stretton* has more character with its clipped hedges, holly trees, thatched porches and black and white of all periods, genuine and assumed. Parts of the village are reminiscent of Grasmere in feeling. The church is black and white and thatched (1903), and there is a fine early seventeenth-century half-timber manor house with an eighteenth-century doorway. *Minton*, 2 miles south of Church Stretton between Callow Hollow and Minton Batch, is a rare survival of a typically Saxon settlement with farmhouse, cottages and an old stone manor house grouped higgledy-piggledy round an irregular village green. A cruck cottage on a stone base, and a naïve sign at Marshbrook Station Inn on the way up to Minton.

Claverley (12). A large village among rich green hills of fertile red sandstone, and well wooded. It stands on a green slope and the buildings are almost entirely red sandstone and half-timber. In the centre is a compact group with the sandstone school, the former fifteenth-century vicarage in well-preserved half-timber and, finally, the red sandstone church itself. This is a large and imposing building with the rest of the village fitting snugly round it. Inside it is very complicated, yet its complexity adds interest as one explores its various parts. The church was founded in 1094 by Robert de Montgomery and the earliest parts date from shortly after that time with additions in the fourteenth and fifteenth centuries. Although there was extensive restoration in 1902, a great deal of good mediaeval architectural features have been preserved and, indeed, it was then that the wall paintings in the nave were uncovered. The early thirteenth-century frieze depicts fifteen horsemen in battle and the composition is reminiscent of the Bayeux Tapestry, though it probably represents the conflict between Christian virtues and pagan vices. In the south chapel is the extremely fine alabaster tomb of Sir Robert Brooke, d. 1558, and his two wives and seventeen children below. Sir Robert was described as "the compleatest lawyer of his time" (see Madeley). There are also three incised slabs to the Spicer and Gatacre families, one of which is a particularly good example of this type of monument. The church boasts two very early fonts, one of which still shows traces of colour. The chancel roof is good work of 1601 but that in the nave is much prettier. Altogether, a very rewarding church to visit. A few yards down the hill is *Pown Hall*, a good black and white house; *High Grosvenor* and *Woundale Farm* are two more examples, the latter with a two-storey porch, open on the ground floor. *Gatacre Hall* is plain brick Georgian, where the Gatacre family have lived, it is said, from the time of Edward the Confessor. *Gatacre Park* is 1850 Elizabethan on the site of a real Elizabethan house. *Ludstone Hall* is a charming Jacobean house by John Whitmore, surrounded by a moat and beautifully kept garden. It is of pink brick with stone dressings and was well restored in 1832.

Clee St Margaret (14). A good stone village in a remote spot near Brown Clee Hill among steep lanes and hilly fields. Nordy Bank camp lies on the hilltop above and there is a ford where the Ludlow road follows

the stream bed for fifty yards. The church has a Norman chancel with a great deal of herring-bone work remaining outside. Opening the thirteenth-century door, one looks straight through a square hagioscope to the altar set against a cool blue E. wall. The pointed chancel-arch is no wider than a doorway. Beside the church is a rambling house with an incredible range of textures—half-timber and red brick, dry stone and mortar-laid rubble, all with a pigeon loft over; the front is dominated by a massive stepped stone chimney.

Cleeton St Mary (14). The road from Hoptonbank is raised above the marshy ground of the common where donkeys graze under the broken silhouette of Magpie Hill. The village itself shelters under the slopes of Titterstone Clee, a cluster of buildings round Nicholson's church of 1878 with its Victorian version of the traditional Shropshire shingled steeple. There are superb views from here.

Cleobury Mortimer (15). The town stands poised in the Rea valley midway between Clee Hill and the Wyre Forest. The surrounding country is hilly and well wooded with good views, mainly to the south into Worcestershire and Herefordshire beyond. The road from Bewdley sweeps down in a great curve over the Rea Brook and into the main street. Everything here goes by curves and different levels; the tree-lined street climbs up and round with good Georgian brick houses and shops on either side and a wide, raised footpath to give a sense of spaciousness. The church itself stands all askew with its crooked steeple and outward-leaning walls yet sturdy enough despite the pressures which seem determined to crush it to the ground. Although heavily restored by Gilbert Scott in 1874, the cool green-grey stone interior keeps its air of calm and peace and an airiness that belongs to good proportions. Once the centre of an iron and mining and paper-making district, the town now

◁ CLUN Castle

caters for foresters and farmers and a little light industry. The charm of Cleobury (pronounced Clibbery) is that there are few buildings later than the mid-nineteenth century, so there is very little that is pretentious or ugly. One of the best houses is the vicarage, opposite the church, a dignified stone house with a trim door and polished brass. Hidden away behind the church is the fine *Childe's School*, a handsome stone building with a hipped roof and white-painted lantern, erected in 1740.

Cleobury North (15). The wooded Burwarton Park extends northwards below the eastern slopes of Brown Clee Hill all the way from Burwarton; a stream tumbles down the hillside through the small village. The church is large, with a Norman tower whose brick top storey and tiled pyramid roof and weathercock were added in the nineteenth century. Restoration was carried out by Sir Gilbert Scott but has left the building remarkably unspoiled. The walls have not been scraped and there is clear glass in the square-topped windows. The chancel and nave roofs are both good and the nave has a parclose screen partly repaired with cast iron. Outside, the church presents a charming picture of the ideal country church, romantically set amid yews and rhododendrons.

Clive (8). The tall church tower topped by a spire forms a landmark which can be seen long before the village is entered. Situated on the slopes of Grinshill Hill, the village huddles around *Clive Hall*. This is Elizabethan (restored) and the birthplace, in 1640, of William Wycherley, the Restoration dramatist (*The Country Wife*). The Church is essentially Victorian though it incorporates Norman and later work. A plethora of stained glass does not really improve it. *Sansaw* is a Queen Anne revival house set among extensive lawns and shrubberies. *John Ireland*, art dealer and writer on art (Illustrations by Hogarth, 1791, etc.) lived here.

Clun (13). The superlative in the oft-quoted stanza referring to this district may be changed according to mood:

Clunton and Clunbury,
  Clungunford and Clun
Are the quietest places under the
  sun.   (Housman) . . . .

It was certainly sunny when we visited the area but Clun is a rather forlorn store-market townlet, set among bare brown hills full of earthworks and bilberries. Many of the buildings have been cheerfully painted but there is an abundance of uninviting red brick villas. An old stone saddleback bridge with irregular arches and triangular breakwaters crosses the R. Clun, and standing grimly on a knoll on the north bank is the remnant of the Norman castle. On the south side of the river is the church, with fortress-like tower, similar to many along the Border, topped with a pyramidal cap interrupted by a clerestory consisting of a line of louvred openings. Inside, angels are carved on the N. aisle roof and there is a good Transitional nave. A pyx-canopy hangs above the altar. The walls have been scraped and much restoration was carried out by Street in 1877.

There are several good Georgian buildings, including the Town Hall and Court House of 1780 and Cresswell Guesthouse. To the N.E. the town is graced by the gables, chimneys and dormer windows of Holy Trinity Hospital, founded 1618, by one of the Howards. It is a single-storied stone building around a grass quadrangle, with wooden lanterns. Well worth seeing. On the right a projecting wing, 1857, including the chapel and with a veranda on round arches. Inside, some original four-poster beds and well preserved old furniture. Sir Walter Scott stayed at the Buffalo Inn while absorbing local colour for his novel *The Betrothed*.

New Invention is a minute hamlet south of Clun with a pretty 1864 *Methodist Chapel*. The bright yellow washed walls of the interior make a pleasant contrast to the dark-varnished woodwork. Good glazing. The inn is styled "the Last in England". The curious name of this hamlet is said to derive from an occasion when Dick Turpin had his horse shod at the smithy there but with the shoes put on back-to-front to confuse his pursuers.

The small *museum* in Clun contains thousands of flint arrowheads, knives and scrapers gathered from the surrounding hills of the Clun Forest. The word "forest" in the locality, does not imply a large tract of trees but rather a bleak, hilly upland which in more modern times has been afforested in suitable areas by the Forestry Commission.

Clunbury (13). A compact grey stone village in the Clun Valley, deep among orchards and overshadowed by the austere lines of Clunbury Hill. The ochre-grey church has a large Norman nave and chancel and a stubby thirteenth-century battlemented tower. A very pleasant interior with a good roof—quatrefoil type—and a fine looking W. end with a Norman font and the back of the 1637 pulpit. Some good lichen-covered tombstones, beside the porch. The Churchwardens' Accounts record that in 1639 lead was obtained from a "plumer" at Munslow and used to cover "the pinnacle of the steple". An unusual "direction pillar" at the crossroads was erected in 1800 by the second Lord Clive, afterwards first Earl Powis.

Clungunford (14). Set in much more gentle and wooded country in contrast to the bare Clun landscape. The large fourteenth-century church is set well back from the road with an almost detached nineteenth-century tower. It is pink-washed inside with panelling from the old pews lining the lower part of the walls in the nave and exposed stonework lower down in the chancel. A plain roof. Altogether pleasant, airy and light. There is a group of three good eighteenth-century memorial brasses set in wood frames, carved and painted to simulate marble. *Clungunford House* is brick Georgian. *Broadward House* is an early eighteenth-century house romanticised by early Victorian castellations. *Abcott Manor* has good timber-framed parts and has recently been restored. *Shelderton*, on the Ludlow road, is a stone hamlet where the road winds up a wooded gorge. *Fernley Hall*, in this parish, was

△ COALPORT in the 19th century
◁ Kiln at COALPORT

burned down in 1856 and was replaced by a brash neo-Jacobean house. The park was laid out by William Kent.

Coalbrookdale (12). In a gorge, where the stream originally known as the *Coldbrook* cleaves its way down to join the Severn. The road from Dawley and Horsehay follows, down winding, precipitous slopes, past looming iron sheds and clay workings. This Dale today has not changed so very much from Hannah Darby's description of it in 1753: "Methinks how delightful it would be to walk with thee into fields and woods, then to go into the Dale to view the works; the stupendous Bellows, whose alternate roars, like the foaming billows, is awful to hear; the mighty Cylinders, the wheels that carry on so many different branches of the work, is curious to observe; the many other things which I cannot enumerate; but if thou wilt come, I am sure thou would like it. It's really pleasant about our house, and so many comes and goes that we forget that it's the Country till we look out at the window and see the woodland prospect." One can still look across the Dale and see dozens of columns of smoke rising in the autumn air against the trees and still hear the clangour from the Coalbrookdale Works, still stand even where Hannah Darby must have sat when she wrote to her aunt, for although some of the buildings have changed the extent of them has not altered.

Darby's second house still stands on the hill up to Sunnyside, with what were the Company's offices alongside. The Friends' Meeting House has gone but the Darby tombstones remain in the burial ground behind. The story of Coalbrookdale is very much that of the Darby family and the Dale Company, or Coalbrookdale Co., as it later became. However, when Abraham Darby I came here in 1708 it was to take over and rebuild the Old Furnace erected by Sir Basil Brooke in 1638 (see Madeley and Claverley), and there were already many other furnaces working. But Darby was the first to smelt iron with coke and from this sprang all the magnificent achievements of the Industrial Revolution. This more than justifies Coalbrookdale's claim to be the cradle of the iron industry. It was there that the first iron steam engine cylinder was cast, the first iron railway was laid (1767), the first cast-iron aqueduct (1796), the first complete metal-framed building (1797), and, perhaps most famous of all, the first iron bridge (1779). "It is possible, even to this day, to sense the presence and influence of the first iron masters and their contemporaries" (Ironbridge Trust), and there appears every likelihood that this whole area will be designated a Conservation Area. There already exists an extremely good museum maintained by Allied Ironfounders Ltd., which includes the Old Furnace site and this should on no account be missed. On a bluff, above the Works, is a red brick Methodist church in the Italianate style and then, perched on the hill-side, Holy Trinity, paid for by the Darbys and with a good deal of cast iron within and without. The forbidding blue brick Literary and Scientific Institute (1859, and claimed as the first college of further education in the country) is but one example of the true Quaker concern for their employees and families shown by the Darbys. Towards Buildwas, the railway which runs through the Dale passes over the Severn on the 200 ft. single-span Albert Edward bridge (1863), designed by John Fowler and cast at Coalbrookdale.

Coalport (12). Now a forlorn and dead industrial area down-river from Ironbridge but still in the awesome Gorge. "From Coalport to Ironbridge, two miles, the river passes through the most extraordinary district in the world; the banks on each side are elevated to the height of from 3 to 400 feet, studded with Ironworks, Brickworks, Boat Building Establishments, Retail Stores, Inns and Houses, perhaps 150 vessels on the river, actively employed or waiting for cargoes; while hundreds and hundreds of busy mortals as assiduously engaged; melting with the heat of the roaring furnace: and though enveloped in thickest smoke and incessant dust, are cheerful and happy." (Hulbert, 1837. See also Hadnall.) The furances and kilns are cold now, though this was once a spot with a long tradition of clay working and there were many small potteries in the area. It was to one of these that Thomas Turner came from the Royal Worcester factory in 1772 and began making porcelain. He was joined at Caughley (pronounced Carfley) in 1775 by Robert Hancock, the principal engraver at Worcester, and thus was established a partnership which has had repercussions on china decoration ever since. The early wares were very fine indeed practically indistinguishable from Worcester and are now, rightly, much sought after. Thomas Minton, who later founded his own works, was apprenticed to Turner, and it is he who is credited with designing the famous "Willow Pattern" here, c. 1775. John Rose, another apprentice, started his own pottery at Jackfield, and in 1779 purchased Caughley, which he operated until 1814 when all work was transferred to Coalport. After many complicated transactions the business moved to Stoke-on-Trent, but the ruins of the old works can still be seen on the river bank where fragments of blue and white porcelain may still be discovered. At Coalport, too, was the inclined plane, linking the river with the Coalport Canal and the Blists Hill Iron Works (see also Madeley). Coalport Bridge (1808) is one of the oldest iron bridges in the world and of very graceful design. The progress up the gorge to Ironbridge is unforgettably beautiful and desolate.

Cockshutt (5). A main road village in unassuming country with a brick church of 1777, with a very angular tower. *Shade Oak* 1¾ m. S.W., a seventeenth-century house with attractive black and white painted brick; the tree itself came down in a gale in 1968. *Wycherley Hall*, 1½ m. S.W., part half-timber, part brick, all in black and white and well set off by lawns and roses. *Crosemere*, a favourite angling spot, surrounded by reeds and marshy Whattal Moss. *Sweatmere*, the least known and smallest of the meres, has an abundance of wildlife.

Cold Weston (14). A farm and a tiny church, accessible only across the fields, nearly a thousand feet up. There are magnificent views across Corvedale and the bare slopes of Brown Clee. Even this small and plain Norman church failed to escape restoration during the last century.

Colemere (5) or Lyneal-cum-Colemere, consists of two hamlets set close together and almost completely joined by a half-mile avenue of chestnuts. On either side are green meadows with Friesian cows. Approaching the church I saw first two sails and then a thicket of masts belonging to the sailing club which now uses the mere opposite the church. Two boats becalmed on a summer's evening on the tree-ringed lake. The church is mid-Victorian Gothic by Street, in

CONDOVER

excellent taste and with a cool and dignified interior.

Condover (11). The village lies in an undulating and well-wooded landscape between Shrewsbury and Church Stretton. The church is a good example of rare lateish seventeenth-century rebuilding after the tower fell and crushed the nave in 1660. The smooth-dressed pink sandstone is rather severe and the main interest lies in the "gallery" of British sculpture from the early Renaissance to G. F. Watts. The memory of the Scrivens, Owens and Cholmondleys is perpetuated in a series of monuments which are colourful, unusual and heartrending. Watts' theatrical treatment of Sir Thomas Cholmondley dominates, but the rest are perhaps more rewarding. *Condover Hall* is undoubtedly the finest Elizabethan house in Shropshire. It was built on a grand scale in pink sandstone and looks out over a tree-dotted landscape, itself making a fine silhouette with its gables, chimneys and towers. In the grounds are formal arrangements of clipped box and yew. A massive gateway frames the view from the road. The house was built for Thomas Owen by Walter Hancock of Much Wenlock, who also built the Old Market Hall, Shrewsbury, and High Ercall. (See also Much Wenlock.)

Coreley (17). The country here is hilly and unspoilt, with cottages, mills, streams and orchards. The once-interesting eighteenth-century church has been devastated.

Cound (11). *Upper Cound* is a happy mixture of Victorian and genuine half-timbered cottages surrounded by gardens with roses, dahlias and Michaelmas daisies. The church is on the edge of the park of Cound Hall and, despite restoration and scraping inside, sits very well in this green landscape. The warm sandstone tower is low and broad, Perpendicular in style with buttresses, battlements and pinnacles. The well-carved door has massive iron hinges and a "sanctuary knocker". Inside is a carved Norman font (fossils in the stone) and several good monuments. The chancel walls are panelled, with excellent Georgian monuments above, marble against sandstone; the best is to Dr Edward Cressett, Bishop of Llandaff, d. 1755. Also delicately engraved copper plates to eighteenth-century parishioners, with skulls and angels. A good early chest. One enters the village over a distinctive little white-painted bridge across the Cound Brook, "Cast at Coalbrookdale 1797". *Cound Hall* is a fine square brick house in a park overlooking the Severn valley with massive fluted pilasters and a heavy cornice. It was built in 1704 for Edward Cressett and is typical of the splendid brick buildings for landowners in Shropshire in the early part of the eighteenth century.

Craven Arms (14). A small but extremely busy junction by road and rail. An hotel and a handful of houses along the main road. Pretty roads lead up from here to the hills of the Clun Forest with its wild and splendid slopes. Church Stretton and the Longmynd are close at hand, and in autumn thousands of sheep

Owen monument, ▷
CONDOVER

70

NEAR this Place lie the Remains
OF ROGER OWEN of CUNDOVER Esq
who not only deserved the PRAISE
but happily enjoy

COUND HALL

are brought here from the hills and lowlands for one of the biggest sheep sales in Britain. For the little railway that used to run from here to Bishop's Castle, see *Bishop's Castle*.

Cressage (11). On the Much Wenlock–Shrewsbury road where it drops down to the Severn valley and makes an abrupt sweep to the left in the centre of the village. The church is by Haycock (1841), with a curious tower and pinnacles that look as if they have been cut out of cardboard. Very pleasant, though, and with a gallery on cast-iron columns and good glass of the period in the east window: purple, red, silver and gold. The pulpit contains some Jacobean carving with the date 1635. It is said by the Venerable Bede that St Augustine met the English bishops here at an oak tree in the village—the "Cressage Oak". *Belswardine Hall*, 1 mile S.E., is probably by Thomas Harnage, 1542, and though little remains of the original it must have been one of the first brick houses in the county (cf. Plaish Hall).

Criftins (see Duddleston).

Culmington (14). This delightful little village beside the Corve is by-passed by the main road up the valley. It consists of grey limestone walls and half-timbered cottages with gay gardens amid meadows and orchard country. The sturdy church tower has recently been capped with an aluminium frame to the spire and the ball on top twinkles in the sun like the dome on an Austrian church. There is still some herring-bone work to be seen in the outside walls, and the narrow, aisleless nave has been carefully explored to reveal many features previously covered by the plaster. An interesting rather than startling building, but worth looking at for the roof alone. At *Callow Hill*, Flounders' Folly (a square stone battlemented tower) was erected in 1838 to mark the meeting point of four big Shropshire landowners' estates. Above *Norton*, 2 m. to the west, is a large Roman camp.

Cynynion or **Rhydyeroesan (Oswestry)** (4). A Victorian church at a cross-roads on the borders of Wales, among near-mountains. The hills are steep with small farms raising sheep and cattle.

Dawley (12). Described variously in the past as "Boom Town", "Ghost Town" and now "New Town", Dawley has been incorporated, along with Madeley, Stirchley, Lawley and Malinslee, into what was at first called Dawley New Town but has been renamed Telford (see Introduction). The towns and communities merge almost imperceptibly, but what is described here is what is still recognisably Dawley itself. The town developed as an industrial centre during the earlier part of the nineteenth-century and its prosperity was based upon the manufacture of bricks and pipes, tiles, iron goods and the mining of coal necessary to support these activities. Gradually, all these fell away and the surrounding landscape of deserted brickfields, mines, spoil heaps and ruined engine houses bears witness to the magnitude of man's labours here. They have a certain haunting beauty still, especially towards evening as the sun is setting, but new roads cutting through the landscape are changing its character. The tidying up and "landscaping" which accompanies them leaves one nostalgic for some of the scenes which were the essence of Dawley. The town itself consists essentially of one very long street, part of the main road to Wellington, with the parish church, a large Perp. building of 1845, away at Dawley Magna. The street is narrow, with no more remarkable building than the Methodist chapel in various coloured bricks, 1860. The area was once a great stronghold of Non-conformism and there is still a vast number of chapels and Sabbath schools to be seen, usually in red, yellow or blue brick but sometimes, as in Dawley, in all three. The monument to Captain Webb, the first man to swim the Channel, in 1875, who was born here, has been removed to the new Civic Centre.

Dawley Parva (12). Towards Madeley and Lightmoor. A Norman revival church, 1845, of red and yellow brick with a stone belfry.

Deuxhill (15). A ghost hamlet on the Cleobury Mortimer road. Behind a good Georgian brick farmhouse lies a ruined fragment of a church. *Hall Farm*, timber-framed and dated 1601, has recently been restored from a dilapidated state.

Diddlebury or **Delbury** (14). A hilly limestone village on the east slope of Wenlock Edge, overlooking Corve-dale. A tumbling stream runs beside the road with a stone footbridge and good houses, set well back. Very picturesque, with the church above, though this is less pleasing inside. It is certainly very old, with most of the structure Saxon and Norman and the whole of the N. wall in herring-bone masonry. It has been scraped, however, and the interior is darkened with poor glass. An exception is the beautiful fourteenth-century cruci-fixion in the top light of a window in the chancel. This district abounds in good large houses of all periods. *Delbury Hall* is plain red brick mid-Georgian in a well-wooded park, and *Broncroft Castle* is Leland's "goodly place like a castle", very picturesque and with fourteenth-century origins but mainly mid-nineteenth-century work with romantic towers. *Elsych* is stone and half-timber Elizabethan, with a moat. All that remains of *Corfton Castle* is the earthworks and moat, and *Corfton Hall* is nineteenth-century red brick Gothic

in a grey stone hamlet. At Westhope is a modernised Norman chapel with old woodwork. *Westhope Manor* is early twentieth-century Tudor.

Ditton Priors (14). A remote village, under the northern slopes of Brown Clee Hill. Good grey stone houses and barns with half-timber and red brick nogging cluster round the church in the centre. On the out-skirts are little rows of cottages and a brownstone Wesleyan chapel with a scattering of more recent building. This was a quarrying community and a mineral line ran down from the hills to connect with the Ditton Priors Light Railway tracks to Cleobury Mortimer. This has now joined the many other fascinating railways in Shropshire and is, alas, no more. The timber-boarded broach spire (cf. Cleobury Mortimer) juts up from amongst the yews and above the very deep roof of the church. From the inside, this roof is an amazing sight in the complexity of its purlins and trusses. Below are some ornate Jacobean-style double seats and good choir stalls. The memorials are good; one of them, a brass to a seventeenth-century vicar, Thomas Jenks, is entirely without punctuation or capitals. Outside, the churchyard has been outraged by clearing the older stones, some of which have been used to make a path, where they are being destroyed by the tread of feet and the action of frost. A barbarous practice.

Doddington (14). An untidy settle-ment straggling along the Ludlow road below the slopes of Titterstone Clee. Its only virtue lies in the magnificent views to the south which sweep from the Clents, past the Abberley Hills and the Malverns right across to the Black Mountains with most of Herefordshire at one's feet. The church is disappointing, with livid green paint and a crude screen but pretty cast-iron windows. *Hopton Bank*. A continuation of Doddington to the east with an early stone-built Methodist chapel now superseded by a much later and much uglier red brick building alongside.

Donington (9). The church is within shouting distance of that in the

neighbouring parish of Albrighton and is set up on a bank above the road. It is a well-kept Victorian building, full of the colours and scents of harvest festival when visited. Other visitors came to receive relief from eye complaints by bathing their eyes in the water from the holy well of St Cuthbert just below the church. There are some good panels of fourteenth-century stained glass in the north wall of the chancel, mainly ruby red, one being especially beautiful. The hammer-beam roof dates from 1635 and there is a poignant memorial to two infant girls on the W. wall. *Humphreston Hall* is a fine Elizabethan timbered house.

Dorrington (11). Like Baystonhill, this parish was carved out of that of Condover, and the church likewise is by E. Haycock of Shrewsbury, following its sister two years later, in 1845. It is a dignified ashlar-built structure, contrasting well with the mainly brick houses and cottages along the main road; the best parts are the tower and spire, the rest is rather dull. Opposite the church is the present school building, but there was a school founded here in 1627 by Thomas Allcock; Richard Baxter and Dr Richard Allestree, Provost of Eton, were both educated here. One of the masters was John Douglas, who later became Bishop of Salisbury and was known as "the scourge of imposters and terror of quacks". John Boydell, the eight-eenth-century engraver and publisher, was born here in 1719 and began his career by engraving prints which he sold to toy shops in sets of six. He invested his profits in new plates and his engraving of Wilson's "Niobe" was probably the first important work of an English artist to be reproduced in this way (1751). He commissioned artists like Fuseli, Reynolds and Angelica Kauffman to work for him and published the Shakespeare Gallery. As a result of his great success, both as engraver and publisher, he became Lord Mayor of London.

Duddleston (4). A scattered parish in the rolling country in the north-west extremity of the county. Many small cottages were built on *Duddle-*

73

stone Heath on unenclosed land in the eighteenth century. At one time there was a thriving brick-making industry here. The church has a nineteenth-century octagonal tower capped with a spire but is otherwise unremarkable except for some monuments and a mediaeval chest carved from a solid piece of timber, and an east window by Kempe. The landscaped park of *Kilhendre Hall* and its house of 1800 are close by, and to the south is *Plas Yolyn*, a handsome Regency house with a pedimented porch. At *Criftins* (Duddlestone Heath), the red brick nineteenth-century church has an exposed brick interior and, again, windows by Kempe. The community here is widely spread along lanes winding over the open farmland. At *Old Marton* there is more variety in the scenery with the Old Hall, a fifteenth-century black and white house, approached by wooded lanes. At *Hardwick* is John Kynaston's "compleat house", built after he inherited the family estates in 1693. It has been much altered but belongs to that fine group of Shropshire brick houses built in the early part of the eighteenth century, (cf Mawley Hall, Kinlet, etc.). To the north-west is a wooded cliff called *Coed-yr-alt*, from which may be obtained some of the best views in all Shropshire. The Dee winds about among the trees below, and its further bank is Welsh. The aqueducts of the Ellesmere Canal and the plantations of Chirk Castle, Bryncinalt and Wynnstay Park form a foreground to the Welsh mountains.

Eardington (15). A small hamlet in the pastureland by Bridgnorth, with orchards and a small Georgian pedimented red brick house, two and a half storeys high, with Tuscan columns to the porch. There is no church. The road to Chelmarsh by Astbury Hall swoops into a deep wooded valley with a lake and waterfall. Of the ironworks, only ruins remain, together with a nineteenth-century red brick terrace of cottages.

Moor Ridding Farm is rented from the Crown for a billhook and hatchet, payable each Michaelmas to the Queen's Remembrancer at the Law Courts in London. This feudal ceremony dates from 1281,

when Edward I granted the land to Earl Roger who was to provide (at his own expense) a horse, a suit of armour and weapons to guard the king on his hunting expeditions around Shrewsbury. As the tenure was held by "petit serjeantry", the earl had to yield to the king annually an "item of war"—a pair of knives. These have now been replaced by the billhook and hatchet.

Eardiston (7). In flattish country, mid-way between Shrewsbury and Oswestry. The private chapel to *Pradoe*, 1860, by Rhode Hawkins, has a reredos in glass mosaic (1899), a memorial to Bishop Walsham How, the hymn writer (see also Whittington).

Easthope (7). One of seven neighbouring communities with the suffix "hope". Easthope is a compact and pleasant village nestling in a fold in the hills on the slopes of Wenlock Edge and looking down into Corvedale. There is a wonderful variety of views to be had from the crest of the Edge, just above. At one's feet, to the west, lies Apedale with the Long Mynd and the Welsh mountains beyond; to the north is the isolated splendour of the Wrekin; to the east and south Corvedale and the Clee Hills. This is close-wooded country on the hill slopes, with Mogg Wood and the remains of one of the ancient Shropshire forests, and it is small wonder there are traditions of this being a spot revered by the Druids. The modest little church replaces one burnt out in 1927 but apes the old rather than starting afresh. The old "sanctuary ring" has been fixed to the new door and a Jacobean bracket which held an hourglass as a sermon-timer has also been salvaged. The original structure of the *Manor Farm* was contemporary with the church and was formerly a cell for monks from Wenlock Priory. In the late sixteenth century some new portions were added and there are some rather unusual round-headed windows. Inside is a fine plaster ceiling by the same craftsmen as were employed at Wilderhope. *Crowther's House* has much the same architectural history as the Manor Farm and is partly of cruck construction.

Eaton Constantine (11). Stands on higher ground above the Severn flats, backed by the lower wooded slopes of the Wrekin. The largely Victorian church is not spectacular yet pleasant, with white walls and dark-stained pews. The blue-painted east wall and altar-frontal pick up the blue of the east window very well. In the chancel is a Gothic organ case and the pew doors still carry brass plates with family names. Richard Baxter, the Puritan theologian, spent his boyhood here in the picturesque Baxter's House. Between this village and Leighton is the tiny hamlet of Garmston, with many delightful old houses, and hardly an ugly one among them.

Eaton-under-Haywood (14). A tiny, secluded hamlet in Apedale, almost enveloped by the thick woods on the N.W. slopes of Wenlock Edge. The grey stone church is tucked into the hill and is practically hidden by the magnificent chestnuts in the churchyard; even the squat battlemented tower is overshadowed. This church is a real joy to explore with its scraped but richly textured walls harmonising well with the mellow wood of the near-flat roof. The nave and chancel are in one, with the floor sloping gently up towards the altar. Where the nave and chancel roofs meet is a tympanum with a coat of arms. The walls are covered with memorials in slate, stone and brass, and even a flamboyant Victorian example in grey, white and black marble does not obtrude here in the gentle light from the clear windows. The pulpit and reading desk are Jacobean and there is an early-fourteenth-century wooden effigy in a recess in the chancel. There are several interesting old houses in the neighbourhood: *Ticklerton Hall*, seventeenth-century, with two dovecotes, and *New Hall*, mid-sixteenth century, a farmhouse with a wall painting of a hunting scene.

Edgmond (9). Looks down from a rise in the land to Newport. Roger de Montgomery gave the Manor of Edgmond and many of the adjacent villages, including "Nova Porta", to his abbey of St Peter in Shrewsbury at the end of the eleventh century. The church and Old Rectory make a very pleasing group at the end of the village; the handsome St Peter's is built of pinkish sandstone with a broad embattled fifteenth-century tower with pinnacles. The chancel roof is steep pitched and complete with gargoyles. Outside, on the base of the tower is an unusual late eighteenth-century lead plaque. Inside, the walls have been scraped, but the colour is still warm and there is much texture. Fortunately, there is no snail-pointing. Pre-Raphaelite glass and a stone reredos obscuring the E. window make the chancel rather dark. There is a good brass to Francis Yonge and his wife, d. 1533, and a richly patterned Norman font. A broad, terraced walk stretches from the church past the former rectory, or Provost's House as it became known early in this century, when Prebendary Talbot was appointed Provost of Denstone College. The house has a magnificent setting in well-wooded grounds which sweep down to the church and village street in a mass of bulbs and shrubs in the spring. Built in the fourteenth century, the house consists of a great hall, with solar and bedrooms and kitchen quarters on one side and a private chapel on the other. Later the hall was divided into apartments on two floors, with lofts above, which may have been used as a tithe barn. A false front with elegant semi-circular bays was added during the Georgian period, and a Victorian timbered gable added in the nineteenth century. *Edgmond Hall*, opposite, is a late Georgian house with a pedimented doorway. *Edgmond House* is fancy Victorian with coloured brick and a pretty gate lodge.

Edgton (13). A tiny huddle of stone and half-timbered houses and farms jumbled round the church on a steep bank between the Onny and the Kemp rivers. The valley scenery here is magnificent, sweeping and surging through wooded slopes with breath-taking views. The little church has nave and chancel combined with a bellcote over. A painting shows it as it was in 1859, and though the box pews and benches of 1631 remain and there are some good memorial

tablets, the charm departed when the "restorers" altered the E. window and introduced cathedral glass and a pitch-pine roof.

Edstaston (5). In flat country, north of Wem, on a disused section of the Shropshire Union Canal. There is the remains of a canal wharf here with warehouses and a stone bridge by Telford. The mainly Norman church must once have been very fine indeed; it is still remarkable for its beauty of texture and what must be the best doorways of the period in Shropshire. The doors themselves, and their ironwork, appear to be the originals. Inside, much of the older work has disappeared but it is still good, especially the nave roof.

Ellesmere (5). Capital of Shropshire's "Lake District". The town existed in Saxon times and derives its name from the mere on its eastern edge. Like many of the towns of this border region, it possessed a castle built in the eleventh century, but by Edward III's time it had fallen into decay and a bowling green now occupies its site. The mere, "Aelsmere" or Great Lake, the largest of the local lakes, 116 acres, is an attractive stretch of water edged by Cremorne Gardens and used for pleasure boating in summer. Two artificial islands are set in the lake and the many species of wild duck and geese attract bird lovers from miles around. Apart from the Great Mere and Colemere, the other lakes are little more than large duck ponds though none the worse for that. With their bullrushes and sedge, backed by ash and alder, they provide a welcome relief to the rather flat country surrounding them. They have no outlets or feeder streams and are well-stocked with pike and other freshwater fish. During the sunny days of autumn the phenomenon of the "breaking of the waters" takes place, when a dark green smelly scum of algae rises to the surface, making the water as thick as soup. After a few weeks it clears as suddenly as it formed, leaving the water fresh and clean.

The town itself has a curious, irregular layout with half-timber houses in Birch Row and Talbot

Street and a number of good plain Georgian buildings. Considering the number of eminent but indifferent architects who have been employed here it is surprising (but perhaps as well) that they have not made more impact on the appearance of the town. The parish church is set on a rise overlooking the Mere and apart from the tower and S. chapel was almost entirely rebuilt by Sir George Gilbert Scott in 1849 at a cost of £8,000. His style was "middle pointed" and he was followed in 1900 by Sir Arthur Blomfield who re-fashioned the Oteley chapel. Fortunately neither of them interfered with the S. chapel roof (Perp.), which is one of the best in the county. It has a very low pitch with carved and moulded beams and rafters and the typical Shropshire quatrefoil panels in the spaces between, and by good fortune there is plenty of light in this part of the church by which to view it.

Oteley Hall, on the edge of the Mere, is a modern house, 1963, standing in landscaped gardens on the site of the nineteenth-century neo-Tudor house demolished in 1958. It fits in to the landscape very well. The Town Hall is a solidly respectable brick and stone building of 1833 with a massive overhanging pediment and there are several other buildings of the same period—the Italianate Savings Bank and Fullwood House. The finest bit of architecture in the town is Ellesmere College, 1879, a Woodard school for boys, designed by Carpenter and Ingelow on an H-plan. The undistinguished chapel is by Sir Aston Webb, begun in 1932. *The Lyth*, an attractive house built in 1819, just north of Whitemere, has a pretty iron trellis verandah. *Lee Old Hall*, to the south, is a very picturesque house of 1594.

Eyton upon the Weald Moors (9). This was originally a low-lying marshy and swampy region with peat bogs, but it was eventually drained. Rushes, sedges and pollarded willows abound in an area well-watered by small ponds and streams spanned by hump-backed bridges. The red brick church was built in 1743 and a polygonal apse added in 1850. Most of the wood-

work is eighteenth century, but apart from some fifteenth–sixteenth-century fragments of glass depicting Saints Catherine and Christopher the interior is stridently Victorian and quite without merit. Close by is the Shropshire Union Canal with the guillotine-type locks typical of this reach. The Weald (or wild) Moors, as the district south of Tibberton and around Eyton, Preston and Kinnersley is known, is not a thickly populated area. The villages stand out as little oases on firmer ground and have a certain affinity with their Fenland counterparts. The sunsets are glorious and the cloudscapes superb over these seemingly limitless stretches of open country.

Eyton-upon-Severn (11). In that green and pleasant land where the Severn meanders down from Wroxeter to Buildwas, gathering strength before the tumble into the Gorge. A gentle and rich countryside with green meadows beside the river and on the quietly undulating hills a patchwork of arable land with the wilder slopes of Caradoc hazy in the timbered distance. The Wrekin far enough away to present no threat, yet *there*, the axis round which all this landscape turns. Pink ploughland with churches to match and a few scattered houses. To the south, Much Wenlock and the limestone. Walter Hancock came from there and it may have been he who built the hall here where Lord Herbert was born in 1583; certainly Hancock was much employed in this area (see Much Wenlock). All that now remains to frame the view are two red brick and stone summer-houses.

Farlow (15). Lies in hilly agricultural country where half of the village huddles round the church on a hill-top while the remainder gathers round the smithy, with a good half mile in between. After an almost alpine, corkscrew approach, there are good views to Titterstone Clee, Abdon Burf and the Wrekin from the churchyard. The much-renewed church (1858) has the remains of a good Norman arch over the door-

◁ Near ELLESMERE
above Blakemere seen beyond the canal
below Colemere

way but is otherwise not very interesting; the red brick Victorian vicarage dominates.

Fauls (5). A church by Benjamin Ferrey, 1856, with a belfry and shingled spire. Also a Wesleyan chapel of 1861.

West Felton (7). A main road village. The church is partly twelfth century with Victorian restoration and the interior is more interesting than the exterior: Norman arcade, good Jacobean chest, some fair glass by Evans and Kempe. In the garden of *The Nursery* nearby is a fine old yew and a curious sundial. John Freeman Dovaston (1782–1854) lived here: poet, musician, naturalist and friend of Thomas Bewick the engraver. *Woodhouse*, 1618, and *Tedsmore Hall*, late eighteenth century, are notable brick houses in the locality. The Holy Well of St Winifred is partially beneath an old cottage approached down a narrow lane at Woolston. Here her body rested on the way from Holywell to Shrewsbury and it became a place of pilgrimage. The water springs up into well-constructed grey-green stone basins and thence, through a pond, into a stream. A still and quiet backwater, with a pleasant atmosphere.

Fitz (8). This is little more than a hamlet, approached along a wooded road with a long range of weather-boarded barns. The red brick church of 1722 is quite pleasant inside although the restoration by Sir Aston Webb in 1915 is less so. By the font are some thirteenth-century tiles and old pew labels have been fixed to the wall nearby. A former vicar carved the Jacobean-style bench ends and above is the original gallery, on cast-iron columns, with a barrel organ. The landscaped park of Yeaton Pevery lies to the north-west, with a walled garden and two domed summerhouses at the corners. *Yeaton* is an attractive hamlet with a compact jumble of red brick, black and white half-timbering and slate-hanging.

Ford (8). Just off the Shrewsbury–Welshpool road, beside a brook in a leafy valley. The church is perched

pp78/79 Two views on the ▷ derelict Newtown branch of the Shropshire Union Canal at Frankton Junction, WELSH FRANKTON

on a hillock between the Mansion House, 1779, red brick and pediment, and the early eighteenth-century Ford House. The church was much restored in 1875. A good quatrefoil roof to nave and hammerbeams in chancel. Two watercolours in the church show it as it was—box pews inside and wooden belfry—wholly delightful and much better than its present state.

Welsh Frankton (4). On the Ellesmere–Oswestry road with magnificent views towards Wales from the road down to Lower Frankton and the Shropshire Union Canal. This was once an important junction of two branches of the canal but the locks are derelict, with ferns and willow herb amongst the crumbling brickwork. English anglers have disfigured this peaceful spot with their disgraceful litter.

Frodesley (11). Close to Acton Burnell, the rather lonely hamlet of Frodesley is remarkable for its lovely views of the hills and its situation on Watling Street. The homely little church was built and added to in the nineteenth century; there is a tiny gallery, some old box pews and a panelled pulpit. The parish registers go back to 1547. Sir Herbert Edwardes, the hero of Multan during the Indian Mutiny, was born at the Rectory. The Old Lodge or Stone House, built by Edward Scriven in 1591, lies high up on the side of Hoar Edge in a lonely, romantic setting amidst the bracken. It has tall, decorated brick chimneys, stone gables and a semi-circular stair-tower with some magnificent mature Spanish chestnuts and oaks on the slopes below. From the Hoar Edge quarries came a type of sandstone particularly suitable for splitting and use as stone slates. The fine roof of the Prior's Lodge at Much Wenlock and that at Pitchford Hall are good examples of their use.

Glazeley (15). A Victorian main road hamlet with stone church by Blomfield, 1875. Norman font in

the churchyard. Brass of 1599. Stained glass east window signed by Kempe. Hall Farm is an excellent gabled, half-timbered house dated 1601.

Greete (17). A hilly landscape with brooks and steep, winding lanes and orchards. The village consists mainly of brick houses and the small stone church has a pleasant, light interior. Restored in 1856, it retains the Norman S. door and in the N. wall of the nave is a late Perp. window with wooden tracery. *Stoke House* is Tudor red brick to which a new front with Dutch style gables was added in 1702.

Grindley Brook (5). An important spot on the Cheshire border near Whitchurch, where the Shropshire Union Canal passes under the Chester road with a staircase of locks.

Grinshill (8). The road from Clive swoops down the Hill and bears round under its shoulder to make a dramatic approach to the village. Conifers and mixed woods climb the slopes, leaving a bare crest of exposed rock. On the far side of the Hill lie the quarries which yielded the well-known Grinshill sandstone; that at the top of the hill is 200 feet deep, though now largely overgrown with birches and broom. From this quarry came the "white" stone used by the Romans in building Uriconium (Wroxeter), and by Steuart at Attingham Park; it weathers to a greenish-grey. Copper was also mined on the ridge at one time. The church (1839–40) was built of the local red sandstone but shows little sign of mellowing to blend with the other pleasant buildings in the village. *The Grange* is a stone house purchased in 1617 by Shrewsbury College as a retreat for masters and pupils when that town was ravaged by the plague.

Habberley (11). In bold undulating country between Pontesford Hill and the Stiperstones beyond. A beautiful spot, little visited, with unspoiled moorland scenery and farms. Ruined and abandoned lead mines dot the landscape. The plain little stone church is Early English but was

re-roofed and thoroughly refurbished in 1864. Two plain Norman doorways survive. The timber-framed *Hall* is dated 1593 and with tall chimneys, but has seventeenth-century additions. It was once the home of the eighteenth-century Shropshire historian William Mytton.

Hadley (9). An industrial area between Wellington and Oakengates. A red and yellow brick church of 1856 by Owen of Southsea, with stone lancet windows.

Hadnall (8). A small main-road village between Wem and Shrewsbury. The N. doorway of the church is the one remaining fragment of the Norman structure and the rest is Victorian and Edwardian. There is a rather sentimental monument to General Viscount Hill, d. 1842, depicting a mourning grenadier and shepherd separated by a lion couchant. One of a family of sixteen children, he was born at Prees Hall and had a distinguished career in the army, serving with Wellington and Sir John Moore in the Peninsular War (for which he received a knighthood). He went on to further distinguish himself at Almarez, Vittoria and, finally, Waterloo, in memory of which a monument—Lord Hill's Column— was erected to him at Shrewsbury. There is a fine set of tubular bells which ring out from the church tower. Outside, in the churchyard, is the tomb of Charles Hulbert, d. 1857, a cotton spinner turned antiquarian, and the author, printer and publisher of a number of standard works on the history of Shropshire. Pedantic and didactic though these works may seem today, they do reflect the opinions of a keen and able early nineteenth-century observer. Hulbert was not reticent about offering advice to local authorities on how they could and should improve the amenities of their parishes and towns. His observations and descriptions of the industrial scene are particularly penetrating and through them we realise how nationally important was the Coalbrookdale complex in its heyday. In the grounds of the now demolished

Harwick Grange, General Hill erected a replica of the Waterloo windmill in memory of his military exploits.

Halford (14). Absorbed by Craven Arms. A grey stone place with an old mill and church above the River Onny, restored in 1848 and again in 1887.

Halston (4). Halston Hall, near Whittington, is red brick, 1690, with additions by Robert Mylne in 1766 (see also Aston Hall) in the Adam style. At the back of the house is a ha-ha with a view across one of the lakes to yew trees surrounding a private chapel, one of two timber-framed churches in the county (cf. Melverley). The interior is very fine, with box pews facing each other and a two-decker pulpit. A helm and shirt with armorial bearings hangs by the altar. It is a pity that the owners of such unique buildings do not receive more assistance with their upkeep.

The Hall was once the home of "Mad Jack Mytton", Member of Parliament, and a drunken, fox-hunting, eccentric squire who squandered a fortune and died in the King's Bench prison in 1835, aged 38. Of the many tales told of him this is typical, and pleasanter than most: "An acquaintance travelling with him in a gig said he had never had an accident when driving in a gig. 'You must be a dull fellow', said Mytton, and drove the gig up a hedgebank and overturned it into the field on the other side."

Great Hanwood (11). A main-road village near Shrewsbury in uninspiring surroundings with a Victorian red brick church with polygonal apse and weather-boarded bell tower, Elizabethan panelling and brightly coloured stained glass. The setting is ruined by the savage lopping of the yews in the churchyard. *Whitley* is one of several townships of an ancient parish which was a detached portion of St Chad's, a bare four miles from Shrewsbury, containing some of the oldest settlements in the county. There were once a number of thriving industries here: flour mills, brick kilns, a soap works, brewery, lime kilns and even a coal mine. These have all gone and only a few ghostly shadows remain to remind one of its former importance. At Whitley the gaunt and angular red brick house, built by the Owens of Condover, stands on the site of an earlier moated building which was demolished to make room for it. It still has a very good date stone with the initial W.O. 1667 and a coat of arms. The inside of this house is Jacobean and far richer than the grim exterior would suggest. *Wellbatch* is another of these townships, with a square, Georgian house with an elegant porch supported on two columns. Clog-making was a flourishing local industry here until the beginning of this century. The derelict seventeenth-century Seveon's Mill (Red Hill Mill), can still be seen near Hook-a-Gate. *Longden* is a sizeable village (formerly a chapelry and township of Pontesbury), with substantial brick barns and cottages and a Victorian brick gazebo at the southern entrance. The brick and stone church was extensively restored in 1877 though the roof is older. The font and pulpit are eighteenth century. At *Annscroft* there is a Victorian red sandstone church with a very steep-pitched roof and wide, raised chancel. This has a boarded roof in blue-grey, lovingly picked out in darker and lighter blue.

Harley (11). The Much Wenlock–Shrewsbury road has been diverted and now passes the village by. The church is by Pountney Smith, 1846, but with a mediaeval tower. Inside is a late fifteenth-century brass of a knight of the Lacon family and his wife in a "butterfly" headress. A signpost on the main road points to "WIGWIG and HOMER", two hamlets approached down a steep lane and across the ford over the Harley Brook, and nestling under the end of Wenlock Edge. From the hill, by Harley, are to be obtained the best views of the Edge itself. The road sweeps down to its foot, turns, and climbs up through a cutting in the limestone supposed to have been cut by French prisoners during the Napoleonic wars.

Hawkstone (5) is the most romantic and beautiful of all Shropshire parks

—a good deal of it open to the public. It has a hotel and a golf course, which in no way spoil its beauty. The natural splendour of the landscape, in which sudden hills are surprisingly contrasted with gentle slopes, called for careful artificial landscaping, and an elaborate scheme of planting and ornamentation was beautifully carried out in the eighteenth century. The house, a magnificent brick and stone Queen Anne building, is in a wooded recess. For long the residence of the famous Hills of Hawkstone, it is now a house of rest and study for Roman Catholic students. The hotel and golf course are by the south-west entrance. Between the two stretch acres of grass valleys and wooded slopes. A long, narrow, tree-verged lake bounds the whole north-east edge of the park. The park's landscaped features have characteristic names: *The Gulph, The Canopy, The White Tower, The Red Castle*, and so on. The best things to explore are *The Red Castle*, a ruin in a thick plantation; the *Obelisk*, with the figure of Sir Roland Hill, Lord Mayor of London, on top; and the *Grotto Hill*, which has underground passages and a wonderful shell grotto, thus described in the eighteenth century by John Salmon:

Thro' rocks of solid stone we're
  led,
  Thro' hills of various form,
Thro' openings, cliffs, which rear
  their head,
  Against the coming storm . . .
Viewing the rocky mantled dome
  In secret shades retir'd:
Her beams of light thro' coloured
  glass
  Bring to the raptured view
The Grotto's freshness, as we
  pass,
  In all their brilliant hue.

The artificial landscaping made every use of old mines and fortifications. The whole place looks highly artificial, but the features are far too big to be so. The realisation of this provides Hawkstone's rich surprises. A day can well be spent exploring the park and relishing the contrast of greensward and labyrinth, rocky crag and woody dell. Alas! many beauties have vanished. A tumbled, tailless, stone lion behind rusty

bars might symbolise them. As time passes here the accent is put more and more on the natural beauty of the park, which is phenomenal. A red-sandstone folly and the obelisk are visible from the road to Hodnet, after one has quitted the park, and the romantic gloom and beauty of the place pervade a good deal of the surrounding country. The darkness of Hawkstone's wooded knolls echoes the leaden sky of an English early summer.

Heath (14). A lonely and remote spot, high up on the west side of Brown Clee Hill, but much-visited for the beautiful chapel now alone in the middle of a field. (The key is at the farm nearby.) This is a perfect little Norman church, quite humble and simple, with neither tower nor belfry, just a plain barn-shape in sandstone, with a chancel and a round-arched doorway. The sturdy walls are pierced by slit windows, high up, and with a bell inside the west gable. The whitewashed interior is stark in its simplicity yet rich in crumbly surfaces and old box-pews and double-decker pulpit. A Norman font and traces of a wall painting grace the nave.

Hengoed (4). The church was built 1849–53 to the design of Rev. Albany Rossendale Lloyd, who also paid much of its cost. An interesting window in the N. transept with a rising sun above foliage and curious inscription. Very forbidding iron gates but a delightfully delicate miniature spire to the bell turret. *Gobowen*—Modern church, 1928 and 1945 in neo-Perpendicular style. Magnificent white painted Italianate railway station with semi-circular booking hall and waiting room; the whole very well kept, for a change.

High Ercall (8). In flat, pastoral country between the R. Roden and R. Tern with many hamlets, but the village itself is on slightly higher ground. The village was of considerable significance during the Civil War when Ercal Hall was the last Shropshire garrison, except Ludlow, to hold out for the Royalists. Great Shropshire families lived here, the last being the loyalist Earls of Bradford. ("The sod of

Ercall is on the ashes of great men.") The early Jacobean *Hall* was built for Sir Francis Newport, 1st Earl of Bradford, by Walter Hanock (see Much Wenlock), but all that remains is an L-shaped fragment in sandstone with brick above. Between the Hall and the church stand the arched remnants of an open loggia. Lord Bradford founded the nice range of plain brick almshouses, set round three sides of an open courtyard, in 1694. The church was badly damaged during the Civil War but was repaired and reopened in 1662 with good hammer-beam roofs to the nave and chancel. There is much good mediaeval carving on the N. aisle capitals and a twelfth-century geometrical Tree of Life over the N. door. In the large churchyard amongst the elms and yews is part of a preaching cross with an eighteenth-century sundial recording the time at Jerusalem, Rome and Plymouth (Mass.).

Highley (15). Situated on a ridge overlooking the steep-sided Severn valley, Highley has been a coal-mining district since 1879 and rows of miners' houses trail inconsequently across the fields. The collieries themselves do not dominate, and those actually in Highley are now closed. The last productive mine was across the river at Alveley; its associated buildings and equipment do not enhance the landscape. *Woodhill* to the north is a typical between-the-wars council housing estate inspired by Port Sunlight but clearly executed on a tighter budget. The parish church of St Mary has a fourteenth-century cross-base with ropework in stone but the interior is scraped and lit entirely with cathedral glass. At *New England* there is a romantic ford in a steep and winding valley, wooded with silver birch and scattered with primroses in the spring. On the hills are overgrown coal tips. Just above the river the disused Severn Valley railway line from Bewdley to Bridgnorth runs through ghost stations now overgrown with weeds. Beside

the river on the valley bottom are picnic spots, camping and caravan sites and a litter of chalets and shacks despoiling what would otherwise be one of the pleasantest stretches of the river.

Hinstock (9). On the Holyhead road between Newport and Market Drayton. Not a pretty or even interesting village. The church has a classical appearance from the outside with the original nave built in 1719 but lengthened in 1850. The tower is seventeenth century but looks much later. The interior has been much restored, though quite simply, with cream-plastered walls. A barge-boarded Victorian vicarage.

Hodnet (5). There has been a good deal of brash red brick and bungalow development in this main-road village but the northern end is better with black and white half-timbered houses leading to the church and Hall. One of the most remarkable features of the sandstone church is its fourteenth-century octagonal tower, unique in Shropshire. This shows to very good effect as the whole building is sited on a little rise overlooking the village. Inside, this large church was expensively restored in 1846, but it keeps its Norman door. The monuments here are many and good, commemorating some of the most famous Shropshire families—the Vernons, the Hills and the Hebers. Henrietta Vernon is remembered by a fine Rococo memorial and it was through her that the link between the Hebers and Vernons came about. Their castle is now no more than a mound in the grounds of the *Hall*, but the Heber Percy family replaced it with a neo-Elizabethan house by Salvin in 1870. This enormous family included Henry Heber, well known as the writer of many popular hymns ("From Greenland's Icy Mountains", etc.) and rector here before becoming Bishop of Calcutta. His brother, Richard Heber, was a founder member of the Athenaeum Club and had the biggest collection of books in Europe. The Hall is now best known for its magnificent landscaped gardens filling the valley below the house, enlivened by a

series of large lakes and pools and making an exciting display of colour and texture all the year round. These gardens are the work of the late Brig. Heber Percy and are open to the public. At the *Home Farm* is the best barn in Shropshire—timber-framed with brick infill, 1619. Three miles to the west is *Bury Walls*, a large Iron-Age fort with triple ramparts enclosing some 20 acres in all.

Holdgate (14). A plain little sandstone village below Brown Clee and overlooking the meadows of Corvedale to Wenlock Edge beyond. The red roof and grey tower of the church are landmarks for miles but all is grossly over-restored. A very fine and richly carved Norman door remains, however, and inside there is an elaborately carved font of the same period with interlace and a dragon. Sadly, all is in a very poor state and damp. The tower of a Norman castle has been incorporated in a farmhouse and an indication of the former importance of this village can be gleaned from the numerous mounds remaining. Not far away is the romantic and haunted *Thonglands*, a moated and timber-framed Elizabethan house built on to an earlier stone house. A phantom choir is said to sing here at midnight on occasion.

Hope (10). A hamlet in one of Shropshire's loveliest valley roads, beside a stream in the steep-sided and well-wooded Hope Valley. The houses are tucked in on the hillside, below the W. slopes of the Stiperstones. The nineteenth-century church is approached across a little white bridge and the churchyard forms something of a miniature arboretum, with some thirty species of trees growing there. Near the school, behind, is a natural arched rock. Further up the valley are the grey waste tips of abandoned lead mines with stark chimneys and deserted engine houses in this bare and silent landscape.

Hope Bagot (17). A local beauty spot in a steep-sided valley, reminiscent of a Devon combe, reached by deep-cut lanes from the Clee Hill–Tenbury road. These wooded south slopes make the most superb contrast to

the bare and desolate faces of the crest of the hill. Here everything is green and luxuriant, with the shingled spire of the church standing secure above a churchyard full of apple and cherry trees. Pale spikes of fir contrast with the deep green of the enormous yew, and a stream flows past the church. An idyllic scene. A holy well, now with a Victorian well head, is reputed to have the power of restoring sight to the blind. The tiny church is Norman and entirely unspoilt. One enters by an open timber-framed porch and finds whitewashed walls relieved by the pale yellow-grey stone of the narrow chancel arch and window surrounds. A place of complete

◁ HEATH chapel

▽ The font, HOLDGATE

serenity. A tablet in the chancel tells of the fate of one of the young men of the parish:

Near this Tablet
Lie the Remains of what was
   Mortal of
BENJAMIN GILES, Junr. Esqr.
   Aged 31
Who on the 12th day of March in
   the Year 1795
In the prime of Life and in the
   Vigour of Health, was
(in consequence of a Fall from
   His Horse)
snatched suddenly away from his
   disconsolate parents,
and from an extensive Circle of
   afflicted Friends, by
the irresistible summons of the
   King of Terrors.

Reader!–
Contemplate the Fate of this
   amiable but unfortunate Young
   Man, and,
"Let Him that thinketh He
   standeth, take heed lest He
   fall."

At Colleybrook Green there are sad remains of brick kilns and nineteenth-century brickworkers' cottages against little red sandstone cliffs.

Hope Bowdler (11). A neat little stone village nestling between hills which are well wooded. Not far from Church Stretton, across the valley. The approach to the church is by an avenue of Irish yews. It was rebuilt in 1862 by Pountney Smith with a square and squat fortress tower.

HOPE BAGOT

Hopesay (13). In a larch valley between 1,000-foot hills, a dark sophisticated place, a lesser Church Stretton, with several fair-sized Victorian brick villas and conifers. The squat church seems almost to have grown out of the hillside on which it stands. It is rather dark inside with a splendid quatrefoil roof in Spanish chestnut. The Victorian chancel is rich and sumptuous in contrast to the simplicity and mellow colours of the W. end and its handsome gallery. The tower has an attractive seventeenth-century wooden cap. (See also Aston-on-Clun.)

Hopton Cangeford (Hopton in the Hole) (14). A secluded place approached by a winding leafy road and lying in the tight little valley of the Hopton Brook in the Clee Hills. The surrounding country, part of the Downton Hall estate, was supremely well planted with oaks and beeches in the eighteenth-century. After some of the Victorian excesses the plain and unassuming red brick church of 1776 is refreshingly austere. The cool, faded yellow and grey-

white interior is flooded with clear-washed light through the plain glass windows and there are dark box-pews set against a brick floor. The large squire's pew has been curtained off for use as a vestry. The chancel has a polygonal apse with painted walls and arch. Painted texts and simple tablets complete the picture but the building is sadly in need of repair. *Downton Hall*, a mile from the village is basically eighteenth-century brick and stone but was altered early in the nineteenth century when the Tuscan porch was added. It has a pretty little rustic Gothic lodge of c. 1760. *Crowleasowes* is a fine late Elizabethan brick house with a large chimney and fancy stacks.

Hopton Castle (13). Set in a hollow among wooded hills, beside a tumbling stream stands the square ruin of a Norman castle, given by Henry II to a faithful supporter in 1165. In 1644 the garrison of thirty-three Roundheads held out against Royalist attackers for three weeks, only to be executed when they were finally defeated. A black and white former

vicarage stands by the side of the road leading to the church, which is simply fenced off in a corner of a field. It was built in 1871 by Nicholson and is rather dull inside, but there is an interesting ruined tomb of the Smith family beside the porch and magnificent views of the slopes of Hopton Titterhill (1,300 feet), towering over the village.

Hopton Wafers (15). The tiny village, set in a well-wooded valley, beside a stream, adjoins the park of Hopton Court, said to have been laid out by Repton in 1803. The three-storied house was originally a superior farmhouse, improved by Thomas Botfield in 1726 and further enlarged and embellished by (it is said) John Nash, in 1812, in Clee Hill "marble". The present church dates from 1827 and is of ashlar construction with battlemented tower of 1770. Some fragments of fifteenth-century glass, depicting an angel, remain in the window at the base of the tower. There is a well carved and gilded coat of arms (of Queen Victoria) on the front of the

86

gallery which houses a small organ. A large relief of Thomas Botfield, d. 1843, points out the beauties of heaven to his mourning wife.

Hordely (5). Set among undulating land with meadows recovered from drained marshland but looking west to the more majestic scenery of the Welsh mountains. Between the R. Perry and the Shropshire Union Canal, which has some good bridges. The church is part Norman with a timber-framed red brick belfry and patterned slate roof. Seventeenth-century pulpit and oak pews, some with doors. Repairs and redecoration 1967. Tudor brick barns enclose a vast yard, part of the old Hordley Hall, home of the Kynastons.

Horsehay (12). An old-established industrial area on the road from Dawley into Coalbrookdale. The ironworks here were started in 1753 by Abraham Darby II, and under the reorganisation in 1797 they were united with Coalbrookdale works into the Coalbrookdale Company. It was then equipped with a heavy rolling mill and forge, a boiler shop and brickyard, and became famous for its boilers. Later the works changed hands, and the Horsehay Company eventually gained an international reputation for their bridges and cranes for the steel industry. The whole landscape round about is churned and furrowed by clay and coal workings. William Ball, the Shropshire Giant, was born here and worked for forty years for the Coalbrookdale Company. He weighed forty stone and had a chest measurement of 70 inches!

Hughley (11). Sweeping down the steep road from Wenlock Edge, the soils change from dusty chalky-yellow to the rich red of the sandstone of the valley, and the waters that follow occasionally flood the village.

"The vane of Hughley steeple
    Veers bright, a far-known sign."

Housman was mistaken, for there is no steeple but a brick and half-timbered bellcote on the church and an octagonal-faced clock presented by the Earl of Bradford when his horse won the Derby in 1892. Inside is a fine, delicately carved rood screen with the entrance to the Jacobean pulpit from the altar aide. The roof was boarded up by Norman Shaw, probably when he was working at nearby Church Preen in the 1870s. In the chancel are some fragments of fifteenth-century stained glass. The *Old Hall*, c. 1600, is timber-framed with red brick and white plaster.

Ightfield (5). In the centre of the flattish, pond-studded hunting country in the north of the county, near Whitchurch. The Perpendicular church is tucked away in a corner of the village and was almost totally restored in the nineteenth century. Inside, there are two good brasses: one to "the good William Maynwaring", 1497, a benefactor of the poor, and the other to his thrice-married daughter Dame Margaret Calverley. *Ightfield Hall* is a timbered and moated sixteenth-century farm with a haunted room. The avenue linking church and hall was allegedly planted overnight by the devil as a result of the loss of a wager between

87

IRONBRIDGE

himself and one of the Mainwarings. This gentleman is said to visit his old home periodically, driving a coach and four. Arthur Mainwaring, the eighteenth-century poet, was born here. His "Tarquin and Tullia", a satire on William and Mary, was originally attributed to Dryden, and he was the author and editor of *The Medley*, the rival to *The Examiner*. Steele was a great admirer of his and dedicated the first number of *The Tatler* to him.

Ironbridge (12). "Here we may say is the mercantile part of the town of Madeley, and here is the focus of professional and commercial pursuits. The Weekly Market, the Post Office, the Printing Office, principal

◁ Allied Ironfounders,
COALBROOKDALE

Inns, Drapery, Grocery and Iron-mongery, Watch-making, Cabinet making, timber and boat building Establishments; Subscription Dispensary, Branch Bank, Subscription Baths, Gentlemen of the Legal and Medical Professions, Ladies' Boarding School", etc., etc. In short, in 1837 Hulbert found this a thriving and prosperous place, owing its prosperity, of course, to the iron industry in Coalbrookdale and in all the surrounding country. The best approach is along the Gorge from Coalport, with steep wooded banks on either side stuck with chimneys and deserted brick kilns. Splendid and awesome even in its decay and best of all in the lowering stormlight of late evening. "The flaming furnaces and smoking lime kilns form a spectacle horribly sublime; while the stupendous iron arch, striding over the chasm, presents to the mind the

idea of that fatal bridge, made by Sin and Death, over Chaos, from the boundaries of hell to the wall of this now faceless world" (Nightingale). The "stupendous iron arch" was the first of its kind in the world, and Abraham Darby had to enlarge his Old Furnace in order to be able to cast its 70-foot beams. It was opened in 1779 after three months spent on its erection without "the least obstruction to the Navigation of the River". This last was a by no means unimportant aspect of the work, since from the wharves along the river was shipped much of the output of the various industries of the area. Special vessels were employed, the now-defunct Severn trows, which were broad in the beam yet shallow in draught and could negotiate the river right down to Bristol where goods were unloaded or transhipped. The town clings to the north bank of

Gatehouse, LANGLEY MANOR

the river in tier on tier of smoky-orange brick linked by steps and steep twisting roadways. Schools, chapels and old workshops jostle each other for space on the crowded and weed-strewn slopes. The yellow brick church (by Thomas Smith of Madeley, 1836) forms the pivot of the scene, poised on the hill above the former Market House and The Tontine Hotel. On the river bank below is a workshop where coracles are still made. There was an earthquake near here in 1753, described by William Fletcher, Vicar of Madeley. "Fields became moveable; nay, they fled when none pursued; and as they fled, they rent the green carpets that covered them in a thousand pieces. In a word, dry land exhibited the dreadful appearance of a sea-storm; solid earth, as if it had acquired the fluidity of water, tossed itself into massy waves, which rose or sunk at the beck of Him who raised the tempest. And, what is most astonishing, the stupendous billow of one of those waves, ran for nearly a quarter of a mile through rocks and a stony soil, with as much ease as if dry earth, stones and rocks, had been part of the liquid element."

The town today is splendidly picturesque in its decline, and it is to be hoped that in the preservation of the industrial monuments of the area this once-thriving community will not be overlooked. Towns cannot become museums but new life and vitality should surely be given to this beautiful place where man and nature have so long gone hand in hand.

Jackfield (12). On the far bank of the Severn from Ironbridge, where the road staggers down from Broseley, and along towards Coalport on the other side. Here is the same rag-ged and derelict landscape of the Gorge, with steep tree-covered slopes and countless cold chimneys thrusting up against the sky. The emphasis here has always been upon the clay industries, and there was a pottery producing the black-glazed "Jackfield ware" from the sixteenth century onwards. John Rose took this over in 1780, together with the Caughley works in 1799, and later transferred all business to Coalport where, under his direction, the well-known "Indian Tree" pattern was introduced. During the nineteenth century a thriving tile and brick industry developed but has now died. At the top of the hill was the Georgian brick St Mary's and many people were buried in the churchyard there after an outbreak of cholera. All is gone now save a few tombstones choked with weeds, although the spirits of departed souls are said to haunt the spot. When that church fell into decay Sir Arthur Blomfield put the local glazed and decorated tiles to good use in his new Butterfieldian fantasy in the centre of Jackfield in 1863.

Kemberton (12). A rather plain village set high up above rolling green meadows and cornfields in the red sandstone belt. The church (1880) is of the same colour but is otherwise not very exciting apart from a Jacobean communion table.

Kenley (11). There are magnificent views of the surrounding hills to be seen from the tiny church, which is itself set on a rise. The village is a mere handful of neat houses, a former school with pretty cast-iron windows and the little mediaeval church with its diminutive but stout tower set in a churchyard full of yews. The roof beams in the nave are massive and the chancel roof very fine. A pulpit with tester and a good Jacobean reading desk. Archibald Alison, writer of *Essays in the Nature and Principles of Taste*, 1790, was Rector here and was often visited by Telford for a game of bowls. His son, Sir Archibald Alison, the nineteenth-century historian, was born here in 1792.

Ketley (11). Ketley and Ketley Bank adjoin Oakengates and Wellington.

This is an industrial area with many ironworks and factories, brickworks and old ironstone and coal workings, a jumbled and irregular landscape, tired and worn. St Mary's church, 1838, lancet-style and quite good, looks out from its hill to the Wrekin, close at hand. Richard Reynolds was a Quaker like Abraham Darby, and in 1756 he came from Bristol to take over the Ketley works of the Dale company. Some twelve years later he was responsible for the relaying of the Company's very extensive system of wagon ways with the world's first cast-iron rails. He married the daughter of Abraham Darby II, bought a half share in the Ketley works and eventually became manager. His son William took over this position and built a canal to link the works with the Shropshire Canal, and in 1788 completed the world's first inclined plane by which boats were raised and lowered from one level to another by means of an iron railway, "the loaded boat in passing down, brought up another boat". No copper coins were minted between 1775 and 1797 and so great use was made of trade tokens; one issued by the Dale Company shows the Iron Bridge on one side and on the other Reynolds' Inclined Plane.

Kinlet (15). A mere scattering of houses between the little stone school and the "Eagle and Serpent", opposite the gates to the park. About a mile down the rough drive which rises and dips towards the hall is the church, buried among trees and on the top of a small hill. (The key is kept at the house beside the school.) This is a very pleasant place, quite sequestered in the depths of the park. The church has a Norman nave with fourteenth-century transepts and chancel and a good timber-framed clerestory. The Victorian restoration by Oldrid Scott in 1892 was unusually kindly and sympathetic, although many of the furnishings are, of course, of this date. However, the chief delight of this church lies in the monuments and in this it is not too pale a reflection of Tong. The tombs of the Blount, Childe and Baldwin families are especially fine and the S. transept takes the form of a mediaeval chantry chapel. Here is the early fifteenth-century

alabaster of Lady Lychefield, recumbent and splendidly garbed in a horned headdress and mantle, her head resting on a pillow supported by angels and the ubiquitous dog at her feet. Peeping from the folds of her gown is a tiny child. In the other transept is the imposing sixposter, double-decker tomb of Sir George Blount (the "Terror of Scotland") and his wife, d. 1584. The lower portion is open-arched with a gruesome cadaver effigy exposed to view. Another Blount, Sir John, in Tudor armour, is accompanied by his wife and eleven children. *Kinlet Hall* was built in 1727–9 by Francis Smith of Warwick, in red brick with stone dressings as was his usual custom, and in his normal impeccable taste. The Knoll, now spelled Knowle, was part of the dowry of Edith, wife of Edward the Confessor. The oaks from here and the surrounding district were once greatly in demand for the building of ships.

Kinnerley (7). A bright orange sandstone church with Georgian nave, chancel and upper tower. The old font with a Greek inscription has been recovered from West Felton and stands near the south porch. Lady Ida's Well, a disused chalybeate spring, is concealed nearby. Close to the village is Belan Bank, site of a Norman motte and bailey castle.

Kinnersley (9). A group of model red brick Victorian cottages here. The church has an unusual double bellcote at the junction of the nave and chancel. The tower was rebuilt in 1674 and incorporates some Norman work and a piece of a thirteenth-century capital. The date of its subsequent repair, 1723, is cut in one of the pinnacles. The interior has been very thoroughly scraped during the restoration of 1884 but the fourteenth-century chancel and arch remain intact. A nice iron tomb (1803) has been allowed to fall into a very sad state. There are a number of unpretentious half-timbered houses in the village but the proximity of the cowsheds does not encourage their exploration.

Knockin (7). A rural village on the Shropshire plain with just one street of attractive houses: mellow brick

and black and white. The church is Norman beneath a smothering of Victorian restorations—the interior is liberally decorated with red tiles, slate, sandstone and buff and greenish stone and there is an ugly and incongruous belfry in yellow brick on the roof. The only remnant of the castle, E. of the church, is a mound, replanted with trees. Its stones were used to build the churchyard walls and the little bridge over the stream. A tree-lined avenue runs out to Knockin Heath where Thomas Elkes was hanged for drowning his ward in a tub of water, having been apprehended while hiding from his pursuers under a haycock in Hertfordshire. Warning of his presence there was given by hovering ravens which had followed him in his flight from Knockin. Ravens are not yet extinct in Shropshire.

Knowbury (14). A steep, high-banked lane leads from the Ludlow road to this quarry settlement on the south shoulder of Clee Hill. The nineteenth-century church is surprisingly large with a stone clock-face carved on the west end of the tower. The random coursing of the stone, glowing a warm orange and yellow-grey in the afternoon sun, and contrasting strongly with the rusticated and less appropriate S. side of the tower, presumably reflects the original work of 1839 and the alteration of 1885. The curious font appears to have been made from an inverted Norman capital.

Angel Bank, on the main road, has a small Primitive Methodist chapel in orange brick with decoration in blue, white and red brick. The paintwork is blue and white; altogether a pretty, toy-like building in the midst of fields.

Langley (south of Acton Burnell) (11). A small stone seventeenth-century chapel stands close to the former Langley Manor House. It is remarkable for its furnishing—the carved and testered reading pew is placed in such a way that the minister must face his congregation at all times, while at the E. end communicants kneel *round* the altar, which stands away from the east wall. Now in the care of M.P.B.W. and recently restored. The gatehouse of

LLAN-Y-BLODWELL

Langley Manor has been incorporated in a farm and is in a ruinous state.

Lawley (12). On the outskirts of the industrial complex of Dawley, towards Wellington. There is a red and yellow brick Victorian church by John Ladds, 1865, and what must be the smallest post office in the county. Apart from the school and a few houses there is now nothing but fields and mounds where once were a myriad of little pit shafts with two or three men mining coal with picks and windlass.

Leaton (8). A church and vicarage in park-like landscape to the north of Shrewsbury, near the Isle (see Bicton). They are both good Victorian work by Pountney Smith, 1859, with a more conventional tower added in 1872. The Victorian liturgical arrangements in this church are undisturbed.

Leebotwood (11). The village lies astride the main road with the church half a mile away on a little hill, shaded by trees and looking across to the Long Mynd, behind Church Stretton. Away up across the main road is Hoar Edge and Caer Caradoc. There are several black and white houses and a very neat, thatched Pound Inn, 1650, with stout beams and some Jacobean panelling inside. The church is especially interesting since it is one of the few in Shropshire which have escaped too severe a restoration. It is mainly eighteenth-century and has kept its plaster outside. In the churchyard is a whole series of uniform tombstones, all to the Corbett family. The inside is well lit with clear glass and the east window has some pleasant glass, possibly by Evans. Some of the old roof timbers have curious carving and there is a two-decker pulpit. Classical pillars form a screen to divide the nave from the chancel where there are some good wall tablets to the Corbett and Plymley families. The hanging monument to Sir Uvedale Corbett, d. 1701, is particularly handsome. In many of the box-pews are whimsical iron hat pegs. Unfortunately, the roof was repaired during the nineteenth-century with pitch pine boards which cry out for white paint, and the Victorian floor tiles strike the only inharmonious note in an otherwise perfect church.

Lee Brockhurst (8). The bridge over the R. Roden on the Whitchurch–Shrewsbury road marks the site, and probably the reason for the existence, of this small village. It is the home of the kennels of the North Shropshire Hunt. The Norman doorway, with its zig-zag decoration, is hidden by a wooden porch, but any hopes which this may raise are dashed by the rather disappointing interior. The road to Wem makes an exciting hairpin round and over the river and in the other direction are the pleasures of Hawkstone (see p. 81).

Leighton (11). A most restful wooded place where the Hall and church stand side by side on green meadows which sweep down to the Severn. Clipped yews and box abound and there are some pretty nineteenth-century black and white cottages with fancy leading to the windows. The Georgian church stands between Leighton Hall and its fine brick stable block with clock tower and delightful row of eighteenth-century cottages. The interior has been considerably mutilated by Victorian restoration which entailed scraping the walls, cutting down the pews and inserting bad stained glass in many of the windows. There are some excellent monuments to the Kynnersley and Leighton families, and within the altar rails is a tomb chest with an incised slab to William Leighton, d. 1520, and his wife. A thirteenth-century effigy of a knight, brought from nearby Buildwas Abbey, was another member of the family. In the nave, the W. gallery with royal arms has survived, and there are two early cast-iron tomb slabs of 1677 and 1696. Outside, by the lych-gate, is a cast-iron tomb with urn to Cornelius Reynolds, d. 1828. There was a furnace here near the Kynnersley Arms (formerly a mill), where iron was being smelted in the sixteenth-century and the ore and coal was carried by pack horses from Dawley and Lawley. The Royalist army at Oxford and Shrewsbury used cannon balls and musket shot made at Leighton. The *Hall* is of red brick with stone dressings, 1778, but much added to. Mary Webb spent her childhood years here.

Lilleshall (9). The village lies away from the Newport–Wellington road and is noticeable mainly for the 70 ft. obelisk to the Duke of Sutherland which stands on a grassy mound at the lower end. The Duke, d. 1833, was a local landowner but is chiefly famed for his monumental programme of road building in Scotland at the beginning of the last century. The surrounding scenery is enlivened by low hills and scattered cottages. *Lilleshall Hall*, home of the Duke, is situated in a huge park, planted

LLAN-Y-BLODWELL

with conifers and rhododendrons and approached from the road by remarkably long avenues of close-planted trees. The house is by Wyatt-ville, 1829, in Tudor style, but its spiky gables and pinnacles are more reminiscent of upward-thrusting Scottish Baronial with its sooty stone. It is now owned by the Central Council for Physical Recreation and their red brick buildings do little to improve the approach. In the village, the church is Norman and early fourteenth-century with a short Perp. tower. The whole was over-restored by Street but there has been

an imaginative attempt to give the interior a pleasant and more lively character by painting the pews grey and by the use of blue and red on the roof. The painted arms over the tower entrance (1657) is really splen-did, but a "CATALOGUE of well dispo'd persons to ye Parish" in-cludes only one name! It is sad that in recent times there have not been more well-disposed persons, for the churchyard has been stripped bare of its tombstones and these now lie against the walls. Some of the best (dismantled table-tombs) have even been used as retaining walls on a

grass bank round the church. It is disgraceful that such good examples of what was obviously a very lively local tradition of stone-cutting, extending as late as 1850, should now suffer such a fate. When we permit such abuse of the churchyards dare we be so censorious of what the Victorians did to the church in-teriors? Half a mile away in flatter country are the ruins of the twelfth-century *Lilleshall Abbey*, standing beside a stretch of disused canal and monastic fishponds. From the truly magnificent W. door to the choir is over 200 feet, but the splendour

93

of these ruins is destroyed by their being buttressed and cocooned with timbers against subsidence caused by the National Coal Board in their operations beneath the abbey. During the Civil War Sir Richard Leveson defended the abbey for the King, and it was during the fighting of 1645 that most of the damage to the building occurred.

Linley (12). A rural parish with a small aiseless church set in an avenue close with evergreens and leading to Linley Hall. This is an Elizabethan stone hall hiding behind a Georgian brick façade. The church is Norman, with unusual recessed bell-openings in the tower, and some contemporary carving within. Otherwise it has been Victorianised. The most interesting features are the carvings over the S. door—chevron patterns—and those over the blocked N. door—a demon with sprays of foliage in its mouth. There is a good Norman font carved with leaves and faces, similar to that in Morville church. The roses at the door complete a pretty picture.

Llanvair Waterdine (13). Like Stow a grey stone village in the Teme valley, set among huge hills where occasional farms nestle in isolated folds. A fine row of lime trees grows in the churchyard, and a holly, springing from a tomb. The church is Victorian, by Nicholson, 1854, and is notable chiefly for the Welsh farm names still on the pew-ends and the boldly carved communion rail with foliage, figures and animals. Just opposite is the Red Lion, with a lively piece of sign-painting. From here narrow and unfrequented lanes wind up into magnificent hills with rewarding views of the surrounding sheep country.

Llan-y-Blodwell — the village of flowers (7). A delightful spot among woods in the valley of the Tanat river, well known to anglers. The hills above the village "command a scene of sublimity perhaps unsurpassed in any part of Wales. The summits of innumerable mountains are seen at once, rising in every variety of ridge, the distant in softest azure, and the near clothed in the richest verdure, with hanging woods,

fertile meadows, and the bright rivers, Vernieu and Tanat, meandering at the foot of the hills, on their way to join the waters of the magnificent Severn. Turning towards England a perfect contrast is presented, in the fertile and expansive plains of Shropshire, richly wooded, and profuse in luxuriant vegetation, terminated on the south by the noble Wrekin, and on the north and east by the faint outline of the distant lines of Cheshire and Stafford" (Samuel Bagshaw, 1857).

The Rev. John Parker, mid-nineteenth-century incumbent, cripple and man of substance, was responsible for rebuilding the church in a highly individual manner. He drew upon every known style of English architecture and added a few of his own for good measure. Although the church is not quite as rich as he left it, it is still a fine example of nineteenth-century enthusiasm and exuberance in church building. There is a good fifteenth-century screen and both pillars and capitals are painted. Window reveals and surrounds are in red and blue and texts are painted on all the available spaces. Stairs in the porch lead to a gallery in the W. end and another on the N. wall carries the organ and choir. The detached octagonal tower with spire carries the text "From thunder and lightning, earthquake and flood, good Lord deliver us" on an arch linking it to the body of the church. Parker rebuilt the vicarage and was probably responsible for the village school (in the lane towards the main road). *Blodwell Hall*, now a beautiful farm, has a fine stone and brick summerhouse in the garden. In the village the narrow stone bridge forms a charming group with the timber-framed Horseshoe Inn, 1445, and cottage alongside.

Llanymynech (7). A plain border village tucked below the steep slopes of Llanymynech Hill and overlooking the Vrynwy river to the Breidden Hills to the south. The higher slopes of Llanymynech Hill are riddled with passages and shafts of mines sunk by the Romans to extract silver, lead, copper and zinc. Limestone is still quarried in the surrounding hills. Ogo's Hole was probably one of these mines although it is variously

described as the place where the British slaves employed in the mine were housed and the entrance to fairyland; it is also linked with a Pied Piper legend. In 1965 a party of boys discovered a hoard of thirty-three Roman silver coins there which were later declared Treasure Trove and are now displayed in Oswestry Library. Remains of Roman fortifications in the hills were probably to protect the mines. The church is neo-Norman by Penson of Oswestry, 1845. The Lion Hotel is cut in two by the border but the bars are safely on the English side.

Longden (see Great Hanwood).

Longdon-upon-Tern (8). There was formerly a wharf here on the now disused Shrewsbury Canal (later to become the Shropshire Union). "Perhaps the most striking circumstance is, that the canal passes over the valley of the Tern at Long, for a distance of 62 yards, upon an aqueduct made all of cast iron, . . . and I believe this to be the first aqueduct for the purposes of a navigable canal, which has ever been composed of this metal. . . . The castings for the aqueduct were done at Ketley, and were removed to Long, a distance of five miles, partly by land and partly by water carriage. This aqueduct was proposed in consequence of the great flood which happened in the beginning of the year 1795, and it was fixed complete in March, 1796." (From Thomas Telford's account of his own work at Longdon.) The brick church is Georgian, 1742, but was over-restored by the Victorians. The *Hall*, close at hand, is a brick and sandstone Tudor Hall, now much reduced but still impressive and welcoming in its warmth. It has some fine brick chimneys.

Longner (see Atcham).

Longnor (11). A small village off the Ludlow–Shrewsbury road, tucked in against the wooded deer park of *Longnor Hall*, a handsome and sub-

LUDLOW from above ▷
and from below

94

stantial brick house built by Sir Richard Corbett in 1670. The neat church set in a grove of trees is a perfect example of a small, late thirteenth-century building with pale pine roof-panelling. Some tasteful eighteenth-century additions include the pulpit, box pews, dated 1723, with bobbin turning, squire's and vicar's pews and a reading desk. Access to the gallery is by an outside stairway. Former doorways in the N. and S. walls are now closed with cast-iron Gothic windows with clear glass. There is very little stained glass and the feeling is both warm and light. The W. window tracery is of *wood* and beside it, outside, stand some enormous tombstones. The interesting black and white *Moat House* is all post-and-pan with, inside, the remnants of the former open roof of the hall.

Loppington (5) lies at the junction of a number of minor roads. Set in a stone in one of them, outside the Dickin Arms, is the only remaining bull-ring in Shropshire, believed to have been in use for bull baiting up to about 1835. Close behind is the parish church, old and mellowed; it is uninspiring architecturally but has an interesting history. It was garrisoned by the Roundheads during the Civil War and partially burned when stormed by the King's forces, one of their rarer victories in this county. As a result, the nave was rebuilt, with a good roof, the carving over the wooden porch testifying to the date: "NICHOLAS DICKIN CHURCH WARDEN 1656." Close by is a rather lonely-looking Queen Anne brick house, and beyond, a pretty, pink-washed half-timbered house with a massive multiple chimney.

Burlton Grange is 1895 Tudor with some genuine parts and nearby is a pretty black and white cruck cottage.

Loughton (14). A farm and a 1622 church, so rebuilt by Victorians as to be unrecognisable. Disused looking.

Ludford (14). The church hangs on the edge of a steep woody hill on the

◁ LUDLOW
  above Broad Gate
  below Butter Cross

main road looking down to the broad stream of the Teme where it washes Ludlow. Ludford bridge is mediaeval and its awkwardness for motorists is compensated for by its great beauty. Above the church is Charlton (Ludford) House, a tumbling mixture of stone and half-timber with massive chimneys jutting dramatically against the sky. It was all freshly painted at the time of our visit and full of sparkle against the dark churchyard yews and fast moving clouds of a sunny spring day. Winding up past some stone almshouses is the entrance to the church. The nave is Norman with a fourteenth-century chancel. The interior has been scraped but this has detracted less from its appearance than in many other churches. The sixteenth-century Foxe Chapel has some interesting monuments but is otherwise dull. Just below the church is a very attractive half-timber house, the Old Bell, and further along the river an old stone and timber mill faces its counterpart on the opposite bank. At Whitcliffe, the Ludlow Arms, another similar building, has its own fives court. The village is an attractive early-Victorian appendage to Ludlow.

Ludlow (14). A charming and much-visited town which makes a congenial stopping place whichever way one is travelling, or better still, a place to visit for its own sake.

> "Or come you home of Monday,
> When Ludlow market hums
> And Ludlow bells are playing
> 'The conquering hero comes' "

A. E. Housman knew and loved this town, and his ashes are buried in the churchyard of St Lawrence's. Of all the Shropshire towns Ludlow has preserved its character as a busy market town and shopping centre for the south-western part of the county and parts of Herefordshire. It is a classic example of a "new town" but new when the castle was built in about 1085–94 and Roger de Lacy set down this "plantation" at its gates. It was laid out then on a grid plan, and this can still be detected in the arrangement of the streets, although later building filled in the High Street and created from it a series of narrow lanes. These narrower, tightly-packed portions make a per-

fect foil to the wide and stately streets on the hill down to the river. The best view of the town is from the Shrewsbury road with the church tower crowning the town like a majestic cathedral at the top of the hill. The best *approach*, though, is from the Leominster road, over Ludford Bridge with its cutwaters thrusting into the raging Teme in winter. First up to the narrow Old Broad Gate and then to the unexpected beauty of Broad Street, lined with Georgian houses, developing further up into banks, shops and hotels housed in earlier buildings rich in half-timber. This street is wide, cobbled at each side, and one of the handsomest streets in any English town. The old Butter Cross closes the view with its beautiful stone portico and cupola by William Baker, 1743–4. Behind, and up a narrow stair, is the Museum with its amazing collection crammed into a tiny space —local bygones and details of the stage coach service to London, natural history and a comprehensive collection of fossils from the Ludlow limestone. Turning left into the High Street (a narrow lane), one comes to what Prof. Pevsner describes as "Ludlow's bad luck", a masterly understatement of the ugliness of the red brick Town Hall. However, the Georgian brick house and Girls' High School more than atone for this and one comes to the castle. This is the epitome of what a castle ought to be, set watchfully on the cliff above the Teme and looking out over the Welsh Marches. The best overall view of it is from across the river at Whitcliffe and for the panorama of the surrounding country you must climb to the top of the tower. Building continued here until 1581, for this was the seat of the President of the Marches and a vital strongpoint in the English defence system for several centuries. Later, it was the last Royalist fortress to hold out during the Civil War (save Castle Cornet, Guernsey). The late Norman chapel has a circular nave, well preserved like the rest, and it was in the hall that Milton's *Comus* was first performed on Michaelmas night in 1634. The church is the largest in the county and still very fine despite the depradations of Gilbert Scott and A. W.

Blomfield. It is mainly fifteenth-century and its chief glory is its setting and its stately tower dominating the town, but it is worth visiting for its woodwork alone. The choir stalls were made in 1447 and are both amusing and interesting. Some of the stained-glass fragments are mediaeval but the remainder is mostly of about 1860. *The Feathers* is a splendid and very well-known half-timbered inn of 1603 (recently renovated), which incorporates every device the carpenters knew, and very fine it is. Less well known is the richly moulded plaster ceiling within. On the Kidderminster road is the basilica-style Roman Catholic church in rock-faced limestone. Henry James summed up Ludlow very well in 1883 when he described it as "a place on which a provincial 'gentry' has left a sensible mark".

Lydbury North (13). In a wide valley on a hill slope just above the River Kemp, where it has been widened to form a long ornamental lake on the edge of Walcot Park and where a small bridge leads into parkland planted with fine beeches. The church is massive and strong-looking, with a fortress-like and well-buttressed tower as befitted its Border situation. It is cruciform in plan with a late Norman nave. The two long transepts are known as the Plowden (N.) and Walcot (S.) Chapels after the two local halls. The seventeenth-century Walcot chapel has some old benches and, set in the floor, memorials to that family. In a little room above, complete with a separate door and a little window opening into the church, John Shipton set up his school in 1663. The Plowden chapel, once used by that Catholic family, was founded by the Crusader Roger Plowden in gratitude for his escape from prison at Acre; it has a high stone altar with stone brackets above (a relic of pre-Reformation liturgical arrangements). The whole church was carefully restored in 1901–2 and fresh white paint and clear glass go well with the rich Border-style roof and carved Jacobean box-pews. There is a delicately carved rood screen and above, black-letter Commandments and Creed, 1615. The timber porch makes a very handsome en-

trance. (Notice the bullet marks on the door.) Next to the church is the *Red House*, late seventeenth-century with Georgian windows and an octagonal cockpit with pyramid roof. *Walcot Hall*, in splendid grounds across the river, was designed by Sir William Chambers for Lord Clive of India in red brick and with the lake in front. On the hillside is a half-mile plantation of trees spelling out "PLASSEY", scene of Clive's victory in 1759. In 1784, Edward, son and heir of Lord Robert Clive, married Henrietta Herbert and thus linked the two famous families (see Chirbury). He was created Earl of Powis in 1804 (3rd cr.). *Plowden Hall*, two miles east, is a good timber-framed Elizabethan house looking across the R. Onny to the Long Mynd. In the private chapel is a brass to Humphrey Plowden, d. 1557, and his wife, in Tudor dress. On the Bishop's Castle road is a pleasant Georgian inn—the Powis Arms.

Lydham (13). In a wide valley, just north of Bishop's Castle, with an atmosphere more Welsh than English. The church was originally thirteenth-century but was restored in 1642 and rebuilt in 1885 to no good effect. The roof is very much that of a Border church, with collar-beams and braces in the chancel and wind braces in the nave. There are some long box-pews and a plain, cut-down, Jacobean pulpit, but the overall effect is marred by cathedral glass and shiny tiles.

Lyneal-cum-Colemere (see Colemere).

Madeley (12). Until a few years ago Madeley was an unspoiled specimen of an early industrial town with brown and yellow brick on steep hills, full of turns revealing handsome mid-Victorian Nonconformist chapels, hall and institutes. Formerly intersected by railways and a canal (now defunct), the town is now torn into by a great new road. Part of the vast new town of Telford, Madeley is changing fast and much of the nineteenth-century character is disappearing in front of the bulldozers

◁ The Feathers, LUDLOW

and excavators of the developers. Though much will inevitably be lost, an attempt is being made to preserve both the atmosphere and relics of the Industrial Revolution in Shropshire on the Blists Hill Valley site S.E. of the town. Here, the Iron-bridge Gorge Museum Trust is establishing the nucleus of what promises to be the finest industrial archaeological museum in the country. Unlike some other collections, this will consist very largely of material preserved *in situ* and will include the last remaining length of the Coalport Canal, ending in the Coalport Inclined Plane, the Blists Hill Iron Works and stretches of the old tramway system. Thus, together with the Old Furnace and museum at Coalbrookdale, one can find a unique and imaginative tracing of the history of the Industrial Revolution in its very home.

Deep twisting roads descend from new buildings to *Madeley Court*, the patched-up shell of a magnificent sixteenth-century manor, gatehouse and all. Carved grey limestone, warm brick, crumbling garden walls, nettles and stone-mullioned windows are all that remain, yet the splendour of the place has not entirely departed. The house was built by Sir Robert Brooke (buried at Claverley), Speaker of the House of Commons, Recorder of London and "the compleatest lawyer of his time", on the site of a Grange belonging to the priors of Wenlock. Standing forlornly in the neglected garden is a 4-feet square block of stone, an astronomical "toy" originally set on pillars 15 feet high (Pevsner). In 1638, Sir Basil Brooke, Lord of the Manor of Madeley, built the Old Furnace (see above), for smelting iron, so it was no mere chance that in 1709 Abraham Darby I made the Court his home until his death. The Nonconformist chapels, scattered so liberally through the town, are examples of the last tradition of graceful classic proportion surviving in England. The parish church is octagonal and was designed by Telford, the engineer, in 1796. It is of stone, now darkened to a smoky brown, with a neat tower and a chancel unfortunately added in 1796. Though the galleries remain, the interior deserves better glass and much better painting.

In the window openings at the east end of the church are the well-weathered remains of what have been four very fine carvings of members of the Brooke family. The churchyard, beyond and below, is magnificent. Many fine Victorian and earlier tombs are in a forest of stone, marble and iron down the hill. There are some unique cast-iron tombs of the eighteenth and early nineteenth centuries, with beautifully engraved lettering and cast classic urns. They are now in a disgraceful state, overgrown with weeds and nettles, flaking and rusting away; they ought to be preserved before it is too late. Beneath one of them lies the Rev. William Fletcher, "a man of apostolical piety and zeal", who was vicar here from 1760 to 1785 (see Ironbridge), before the present church was built on the site of the old one. William Fletcher was a friend of John Wesley, who wrote his Life, and had he not pre-deceased Wesley he would probably have taken Wesley's place as leader of the Methodists. Fletcher was appalled at the vice of the workers who were then thronging to his parish to work in the iron-works, but he was unafraid of them. At five in the morning on the Lord's Day he would go round his parish ringing a bell at the doors of the houses to remind people to come to church. Miraculous events and dispensations of providence threaded his life through. He was of Swiss parentage (Fléchère), and enlisted in the army for service in the Brazils, but he scalded his leg at breakfast and was unable to board the boat, and so, by God's foresight, remained in Europe to become a powerful minister of the Word. His death was lamented by thousands and he lies buried where he worked so hard. Perhaps the most ambitious building in Madeley is the Anstice Memorial Club and Institute, built in 1869 in red brick by a London architect, John Johnson. It is a building in the grand Italianate manner and, while not very beautiful, it is claimed as the first working-men's club. From 1825 to 1840 Thomas Randall, a former apprentice at the Caughley China Works, owned a small porcelain factory at Madeley and produced a soft paste of excellent quality in the Sèvres style.

MADELEY COURT

Since he never used a mark, authenticated examples of his work are rare, but the quality of Randall's workmanship "rivalled Billingsley in producing the loveliest porcelain ever made in England" (S. W. Fisher).

Sutton Hill and Woodside are the first residential areas to be built as part of the new town of Telford and lie to the E. and W. of Madeley respectively. At Woodside, while individual houses may be pleasant enough (and they all appear identical), the total appearance of their mass on the hillside is an utter abomination. They are densely packed together and have been placed in such a way as to form completely unbroken lines against the sky. Each house is of uniform pink-grey brick and grey tiles and it is difficult to imagine anything more depressing. At Sutton Hill there is slightly more variety of colour and texture but the materials are such that they will hardly mellow in two or three lifetimes. It is nothing short of a tragedy

that, with such vital and stimulating landscape all round, its lessons and examples should have been so perversely ignored. This is not townscape, it is pure tedium. Look across from Sutton Hill to Madeley church if you have any doubts.

Mainstone (13). Lies tucked deeply in the upper valley of the R. Unk. The church is up another valley a mile to the W., under the slopes of Edenhope Hill, where Offa's Dyke descends from the skyline to cross the road between the church and a few isolated cottages. The settlement probably originated as a trading post on the Dyke, but today it is remote and silent, closed in by sombre hills surmounted by prehistoric remains. A huge boulder, from which the village takes its name, is said to have been used as a test of strength. The church is almost entirely late Victorian save for the good black and white roof.

Malinslee (12). An industrial landscape with brickfields and worked-out coal mines. The countryside is gradually being reclaimed for agriculture after the open-cast mining of coal. The church is octagonal, with a W. tower, in massive blocks of ashlar, designed by Thomas Telford in 1805. It is very similar to his church at Madeley and although it has lost much of its character it has fared better than Madeley and is at least light inside. At Dawley Bank is a surprising Baptist Church, 1860, with an incredible blue brick gable.

Market Drayton (6). A fair-sized red brick and half-timbered town on a hill with the church making a fine landmark on the skyline from the south. Entering the town is something of a disappointment, for everything has an air of being abandoned and

MADELEY COURT, ▷
The garden

neglected. This is a great pity because there are some good Georgian brick houses and a former Congregational chapel, 1778, and plenty of seventeenth-century half-timbered houses. The best of these are what are now a National Westminster Bank and Sandbrook's Vaults. The parish church of St Mary was done up in a handsome Renaissance style in 1786 but was spoiled in 1884 and later so that outside, at least, it looks totally Victorian. Clive of India was educated at the old grammar school here (founded in 1558 by Sir Rowland Hill, Lord Mayor of London). The Battle of Blore Heath was fought outside the town in 1459, a Lancastrian defeat. The district north of Market Drayton and extending into Staffordshire and Cheshire is pitted with small ponds which are in almost every field. From the air the sight is extraordinary. *Betton* (the name of several unimportant places in this county) is a hamlet near here in a region of small pools. It has several decent hunting boxes, and a cottage where Queen Margaret sheltered after the Battle of Blore Heath. *Tunstall Hall*, 1½ miles north-east, is a substantial red brick house of c. 1723, close by the River Tern. It has recently been restored to some of its original splendour after serving as a school for some years.

Marton (10). A hamlet in the Rea Brook valley, near Chirbury. Marton Pool—a 40-acre lake frequented by anglers. A small Victorian church with a blue painted porch and simple but pleasant interior. Dr Thomas Bray, eighteenth-century cleric born at Marton Crest, was the originator of the Society for Promoting Christian Knowledge, and, while on a mission to Maryland on behalf of the Bishop of London, founded the Society for Propagating the Gospel.

Mawley Oak (15) has the best postwar house in the county. *Mawley Hall*, 1730, is a fine large house in red brick and sandstone set in landscaped parkland, very English, with magnificent views in all directions. The exterior is simple and unassuming, contrasting with the richness and

◁ MADELEY Church,
   by Thomas Telford

intricacy of the plasterwork of the entrance-hall, the unique carving of the staircase and the inlaid veneers of one of the ground-floor rooms. The dining room was redecorated later in the eighteenth century in the Adam style. Close by the house, grouped round courtyards, are the attractive servants' quarters and coach house, the latter capped with a clock-tower turret. Probably by Francis Smith of Warwick, who also built Kinlet Hall and Berwick. The house has recently been restored, sparing no expense, a great credit to its owner. The view from the west, beyond Cleobury Mortimer, is one which might very well have been painted by Constable—

MINSTERLEY

pale pink house in the sunlight, against elm trees, on a hillside.

Melverley (7). A splendid setting amid green meadows sweeping down to R. Vyrnwy as it flows in an arc to join the Severn. A church and a few cottages look across to the Breidden hills topped by Rodney's Pillar. The sixteenth-century church, on the river's edge, with ancient yews in the churchyard, is an impressive picture of solidity, built of oak timbers, black and white, both inside and out. This is one of two timber-framed churches in the county (cf. Halston) and is more evocative of a barn than a church. Even the nineteenth-century restorers failed to destroy

its robust beauty. A derelict halt of the long-abandoned Shropshire and Montgomeryshire Light Railway remains nearby.

Meole Brace (8). A red brick suburb of Shrewsbury with a very few old houses. Mary Webb was married in Haycock Junr.'s church of 1867, a very imposing rock-faced sandstone building for what was then only a small village. What is important about this church is the stained glass, almost all by Morris & Co., and some of the best ever designed by Morris himself and Burne-Jones. In the apse are three windows: in the centre, the Crucifixion with the Virgin seated below, and to the left and right, Apostles, Kings and Martyrs, all in rich and glowing colours yet clear, with a sense of the light coming *through* the glass and not in the least harsh.

Middleton (N.E. of Ludlow) (14). Leafy lanes full of Queen Anne's lace lead to a small Norman chapel in pink sandstone with slit windows in massively thick walls. A fine, restored rood screen and loft dominate the tiny interior, which has plain cream-painted walls and a scraped chancel. An open-sided porch leads to the close-mown churchyard with its clipped yews and rhododendrons. Middleton Court lies behind.

Middleton-in-Chirbury (10)—lonely and remote, standing high on the W. slopes of Stapely Hill, close to the Montgomeryshire border. There is ample evidence all about of the presence of prehistoric man: stone circles, Mitchell's Fold, a huge enclosure with standing stones, the Whetstones and Marsh Pool Circle (Bronze Age), where there are many standing stones, almost buried in the gorse, encircling a "King" stone. The church is Victorian and full of the work of a vicar of Fitz of the early part of this century. He was a talented woodcarver and stonemason and his carvings include highly individual, and often whimsical, interpretations of local legends associated with Mitchell's Fold.

Middleton Scriven (15). A smiling, open village among trees set in unexpected downland a mile off the Cleobury Mortimer road. The church is unremarkable Victorian of 1848, the prettiest part being the barge-boarding of the porch. *Dingle Lake*, a pond, lies in a hidden, wooded valley ½ mile to the north.

Milson (18). A pretty village amid gentle hills with apple and damson orchards on the slopes. The houses are of mellow brick (one has an intriguing iron spiral stairway on the end wall) and black and white, all with trim gardens. The stone church is Norman with a thirteenth-century tower, shingle-tiled at the top, with a pyramid roof and a good early wooden porch, open at the sides. Inside it is light and welcoming despite the scraping; the pulpit is Elizabethan. Opposite is a large farm with fine brick chimneys, once the manor house.

Minsterley (10). A largish village where the narrow Hope valley opens out into the wider plain of the Rea Brook. A beautiful and unusual brick and stone church of 1689 built by the Thynne family, who moved to Ministerley Hall when Caus Castle (on the Shropshire slopes of Long Mountain, near Westbury) was dismantled. Naïve treatment of semi-classical, semi-baroque motifs with delightfully unexpected touches of whimsey—carved cherubs' heads on the keystones of the arched windows on the tower, garlanded pilasters, carved skull and crossbones, cherubs and hourglass on the W. doorway. The pulpit has an enormous domed sounding board, the dark woodwork well set off by the pale blue-washed walls. Several Maidens' Garlands hang above the pillared W. gallery (cf. Astley Abbots). A splendid setting of yews and conifers with a view of the well-restored Minsterley Hall, black and white, behind. Late nineteenth-century Acacia House opposite and a former Toll House beyond.

Monkhopton (12). Just off the main road with a brook running through. The place has an air of melancholy with trees shading the orange-ochre rendered church with its slim tower (1835). Across the road is a splendid avenue of Wellingtonias and close-clipped grass in the grounds of a private house where a water garden splashes its way down the hill between the trees. Inside the rather gloomy church is a brass rescued from the now-closed church at Upton Cressett. On Tittenhope Hill buzzards can be seen. At Great Oxenbold, incorporated in a farm, are the remains of a house belonging to the Priors of Wenlock.

Montford (8). A village lying along the Severn, which is crossed by a fine red sandstone bridge of three arches carrying the A.5, Holyhead road. Probably Telford's first masonry bridge, 1790. A small red sandstone church of 1737, on a hilltop, restored, and spoilt, in 1884. Near the tower are buried Dr Robert Waring Darwin (son of Erasmus Darwin and father of Charles) and his wife Susan (née Wedgwood, daughter of Josiah), and several daughters. Preston Montford Hall—a handsome early eighteenth-century two-storey red brick house, now a Field Studies Council Centre.

More (13). In a flat, wooded landscape surrounded by the not-too-distant hills near Bishop's Castle, secluded but not isolated. A few cottages and farm buildings, black and white half-timber, cluster together to make an angular group with the church. This has a squat, fortress-like mediaeval tower of the "Border" type, with a double pyramid cap. The rest of the church is a good example of Victorian rebuilding in the Early English or lancet style of 1845, though stripped of the interior fittings which help to make that style acceptable. The little W. gallery is supported on cast-iron columns, and in the More chapel, 1640, a monument to Harriet More with the pious inscription "I know that my Redeemer liveth". In front is a brass with the coat of arms of Richard More. *Linley Hall*, a mile away on the slopes of Linley Hill, is the home of the More family. This is a typically square stone house of 1742, in the Palladian manner, by Henry Joynes, Surveyor of Kensington Palace, and apart from its intrinsic merit it is interesting in being the first of its kind in

MORE Church
outside and inside

Shropshire. It has an elegant stable
block and a charming little picturesque lodge; on an island in a lake
beside the house is a little classical
temple. Robert More was an eighteenth-century botanist and friend
of Linnaeus; in 1738 he brought
back the first larches to England and
planted them here in the park. The
More family claims descent from one
Richard, who came over with
William the Conqueror, and the
family still continues in its Shropshire home.

Moreton Corbet (8). Shawbury
airfield has shattered the calm of this
place, yet it is still one of the most
interesting and exciting places to
visit in the whole of the county.
The grey stone ruins of Moreton
Corbet Castle stand up with great
splendour from the surrounding
flat meadows, almost flat and making
a superb silhouette with the ogee-
shaped gables clear-cut against the
sky. It is incredible not that so much
is left standing but that this shell
should stand at all. Rooks wheeling
about it on a stormy day give it an
air so romantic that one could almost

believe it to have been contrived as a stage set for a melodrama. Not that there is anything melodramatic about the building itself; it is good Elizabethan work with the classical elements coming in with the Tuscan and Ionic columns about which the whole S. façade is articulated. A gentle play of bays and recesses creates life and colour without actual recourse to anything approaching a multiple E-plan. This work was begun by Sir Andrew Corbet, d. 1579, and carried on by his son Robert, so it would seem that Camden was mistaken in his attribution of the work but perhaps less so in the motive: "Moreton Corbet, a castle of the Corbets where, within memory, Robert Corbet, who had a passion for building, began a magnificent house that he might live more splendidly, and at his ease." Enough still remains to make this almost as impressive a ruin as Kirby Hall. The Castle is justly named since there are ruins of a Tudor castle with a Norman keep which were dismantled by Cromwell. In the village, beside the black and white rectory, is the church where many of the Corbets are buried (see also Leebotwood), with some good monuments. Especially worth looking at are those to Sir Richard, d. 1513, and his wife—a fascinating group of painted shields—and two good eighteenth-century memorials

to other members of the family. The church is mainly fourteenth century, with a later tower, but the most striking part is the Norman chancel which Sir Ninian Comper decorated at the beginning of the century with a staggering richness of colour and pattern. *Acton Reynald* is a Victorian stone mansion incorporating early seventeenth-century fragments of another Corbet home.

Moreton Say (6). A leafy village in the dairy pastures near Market Drayton. From outside the church appears to be of eighteenth-century red brick, but this is merely a refacing of 1788 to bring the nave in keeping with the tower which had been rebuilt nineteen years earlier. Inside is what remains of the stone church of c. 1200, spoiled at the beginning of this century but well cared for and the very essence of the English parish church when decked out for the Harvest Thanksgiving. A large stairway with Jacobean balusters leads to a fine west gallery. A tablet tells that Arthur Sandford gave the timber and Lady Jane Grovenor paid £10 for its erection in 1634. Jane Vernon is shown lying between the effigies of her two husbands on their tomb. Robert, Lord Clive, d. 1774, victor of Arcot and Plassey and "Primus in Indis", is buried in the church. He was born near here at *Styche Hall*, and Clive had Sir

William Chambers, "the chaste architect of Somerset House," build the present house about 1762 on the site of the former one, before moving to Walcot (see Lydbury North). There are a number of tablets and tombs of the Clive family here. *Shavington Hall* is in the parish, but see Adderley.

Morville (12). One of the most beautiful main-road villages in Shropshire, grouped round the school, the church and the hall. Approaching from Bridgnorth, the gilded domes of *Morville Hall* rise above cornfields, and then as one descends the hill the whole picture is revealed. The grey limestone hall is set about three sides of a large lawn with a ha-ha to provide an unbroken view of the church in front. Behind, a thickly-wooded hill sweeps up and away to Upton Cressett and makes a perfect backdrop for church and hall. The hall was rebuilt from an Elizabethan house during the eighteenth century (Wm. Baker—Ludlow Butter Cross—worked here in 1748–9), but the feeling for space and modest assertiveness belong entirely to the latter period. The projecting wings and the detached blocks with their domed and gilded lanterns topped with weathercocks make this a minor masterpiece. The church is Norman and Transitional, well Victorianised but full of charm, and

MORETON CORBET Castle

MORVILLE

an archaeologist's paradise with its
Norman font, fourteenth-century
glass and other relics. In the churchyard is a pathetic little earthenware
tombstone to a child. The school is
a good example of original Victorian
work, rich in texture and one of a
number in this county.

Aldenham Park, like Morville
Hall, is earlier than it looks. This
mainly early-Victorian stone house
was rebuilt in 1691 and there are
still parts of that date. A fine
avenue with delicate and intricate
gates leads to this home of the Acton
family. ("All power tends to corrupt:
absolute power corrupts absolutely.")
Father Ronald Knox lived here for
the duration of the Hitler war,
making his translation of the Bible.

Munslow (14). The main road here
is misleadingly dull, but turn off to
the left, where a little lane twists
and curls among steep little hills, and
you will come to the church in a
hollow. Yews and Scotch fir fill the
churchyard and in late spring
myriads of wild flowers carpet the
ground. The dignified late Georgian
rectory beside the church is backed
by beeches and, in front, lawns lead
down to a little lake. By the roadside
are some fine barns and these, like
the church and rectory, are all in the
greenish Wenlock limestone, still

quarried not far from here. The
setting of the church and its superb,
but weathered, timber porch create
a deceptive air of "picturesque
decay". Inside all has been scraped,
tiled and furbished up, but in the
vestry is a charming water-colour
(1856) of the interior before it was
"restored". The church is worth
seeing if only for the glass. The E.
window is a Gothic composition,
c. 1835, in the old tradition of
window staining. In the N. aisle are
three windows of sixteenth-century
glass, very well restored and set with
c. 1840 glass in a way which would
deceive even an expert. The tracery
of some of the windows of this aisle
is remarkably elaborated curvilinear.
By the S. door is a window of pieces
of old glass of various dates; some
early Victorian. Some bench ends
have unusual geometric tracery.

Midway between Munslow and
Diddlebury, and still in Corvedale,
is *Aston Munslow*, a hamlet of black
and white cottages and the Swan
Inn. *Aston Hall* is a handsome early
seventeenth-century stone house with
good brick chimneys, and then there
is the *White House*, a fascinating
puzzle for the archaeologist. The
present building consists of a fourteenth-century mediaeval hall of
cruck construction on to which has
been built a sixteenth-century cross-

wing. Finally, in the eighteenth
century, there were further additions
including a hanging staircase. It
now houses the fascinating Country
Life Museum established by Miss
J. C. Purser and open during the
summer months. On the road to
Rushbury is *Millichope Park*, a fine
piece of classical work by Edward
Haycock, 1840, approached by a
long avenue and fronted by lake and
a rotunda. At *Upper Millichope*, in
splendid country with light-coloured
limestone soil and reminiscent of the
Cotswolds, is a fourteenth-century
stone tower-house with a timber-
framed top storey.

Myddle (8). A pleasantly scattered
village, the houses very red in the
very green landscape. The church
was "remodelled" in 1744 and
thoroughly Gothicised twice in the
nineteenth century but has a fine
tower (1634) with a hexagonal clock-
face. A slender stair turret is all that
remains of *Myddle Castle*, built by
Lord Lestrange of Knockin and
crenellated "by licence" in 1307.
Myddle has the distinction of
possessing a local historian, Richard
Gough, 1635–1723. In his *Antiquities
and Memoirs of the Parish of Myddle*
he relates the history of every family
in the parish with unsparing, and
often unflattering, detail, exposing

At Neen Sollars

many skeletons in family cupboards. His book was first published in the early nineteenth century and has recently (1968) been reprinted. There are some interesting references to the impact of the Civil War on isolated settlements such as Myddle, and Gough gives a very clear picture of contemporary life in such towns as Shrewsbury, Oswestry and Ellesmere.

Myndtown (14). A dramatic setting, tucked down at the foot of the steepest cliffs of the Long Mynd and looking out on a magnificent panorama of hills. A farm, the roughcast church and a few houses make up all there is, but it is the setting which counts here. A mile and a half to

◁ Fourteenth-century glass,
Morville

the north is *Asterton*, similarly situated and with a *very* steep, almost alpine, road climbing up to the Portway, the ancient track which follows the backbone of the Long Mynd. This makes an excellent starting point from which to explore this wild and beautiful place on foot, but remember the fate of the rector of Woolstaston! At the weekends the graceful gliders of the Midlands Gliding Club can be seen hovering overhead.

Nash (17). In the rich, orchard country below the Clee Hills and leading down to Tenbury Wells. The church was severely Victorianised after it became a separate parish in 1849. Seen from the churchyard is *Nash Court*, a good Georgian red brick house with a stable block and cupola. *Court of Hill* is a very fine

brick house of 1683 with stone trimmings. There is an octagonal dovecote with a delightful lantern within well-wooded grounds.

Neen Savage (15). Only a mile north of Cleobury Mortimer but languishing in solitude among the hills and trees by the Rea Brook, which is crossed here by a ford. Papermaking was once a thriving local industry, using the soft waters of the stream, but the mills have long since closed. The tower of the little Norman church was damaged by fire in 1825 and the rest of the church was thoroughly restored at the end of the century. The fifteenth-century style screen, also damaged during the fire, still retains some of the original tracery and much of the roof appears to be original. The hard cement rendering of the walls gives a cold feeling to

109

what is otherwise a very spacious-seeming church. *Detton Hall* is an early seventeenth-century stone and timber-framed house.

Neen Sollars (18). A charming spot, nestling amongst pine-planted hills and surrounded by orchards in the steep valley of the R. Rea, where the half-timbered cottages have trim, well-tended gardens. The red sandstone church is early fourteenth century with a crossing tower and later shingled spire, but has been very harshly treated. The Conyngsby monument is a fine alabaster memorial to Humphrey Conyngsby, d. 1624, "a perfect scholar by education and a great traveller by his own affections". He certainly was a great traveller and it is well worth reading the long account of his life and journeys on the monument.

Neenton (15). An undistinguished and undisturbed main-road hamlet by the R. Rea. The pink sandstone

church by Sir Arthur Blomfield, 1871, is built on an earlier foundation. A good Norman font remains.

Great Ness (8). A compact and pleasant village set among hills with some good Georgian houses and a large red sandstone church. A black and white roof and gallery with organ over late eighteenth-century pews. The tower is very substantial: large irregular blocks of sandstone of a beautiful pink and orange colour. *Great Ness House* has a columned porch and interesting coach house. *Nesscliffe Hill*, a wooded sandstone height overlooking the village, has two ancient camps and a cave reputed to be the hideaway of Humphrey Kynaston, a fifteenth-century outlaw, a Shropshire man "as of the great outlawe Robin Whood" (Gough), who is said to have leaped the Severn at Montford when the Sheriff's officers had removed the planks of the bridge to trap him.

Little Ness (8). Fine views of the surrounding country from the churchyard and nearby castle mound. The church is basically Norman but much renewed. There is a sixteenth-century German or Flemish Triptych: Crucifixion, St Christopher, St Catherine. *Adcote House* (now a girls' school) between the village and the river, is a large warm-coloured stone house of 1879 by Norman Shaw. The massive S. front has buttress and an oriel window reaching practically to the eaves, with Elizabethan gables above. Inside is a lofty hall with an enormous fireplace, minstrels' gallery and fine stone arches to carry the roof. The whole is characteristic of Shaw and set in well-kept wooded grounds.

Newcastle (13). A grey stone village standing where the Folly Brook joins the Clun river, amid towering hills. The bellcote church by Haycock, 1848, is built on a high bank away from the village. It has an ingenious

Adcote House, LITTLE NESS

NEWPORT

and unusual revolving lych-gate. *Fron Camp* is an earthwork on a prominent hill to the N., while to the E., at Whitcott Keysett is an 81-foot menhir. A fine section of Offa's Dyke runs along the hill, E. of the church.

Newport (9). A brisk little market town on the eastern borders of the county. Its charter was granted in the twelfth century by Henry I, and the town's coat of arms, incorporating three fishes, reflects the ancient duty of the townsfolk to provide the king's court with fresh fish, caught mainly in the local meres. This largely unspoilt town was almost completely rebuilt after a disastrous fire in 1665, and the surrounding country is peaceful yet unremarkable. There are few industries here of other than local importance; agricultural engineering, timber yards and saw mills specialising in high quality English oak for interior decoration. The hub of the town lies in its one spacious and dignified street, High Street, bending roughly N. to S. and rising gently from a disused section of the Shropshire Union Canal. The parish

church is on an island site in the centre of the street. Many inns, dignified Georgian houses (often with cobbled forecourt and decorative eighteenth-century ironwork), Victorian houses and decent, sober shops catering for the needs of the district, line this thoroughfare. There are few outstanding buildings from an architectural point of view but there are several that are interesting. Probably the most resplendent is the Royal Victoria Hotel, c. 1830, with its Tuscan porch and pilasters, all very nicely painted. Almost opposite, Adams' Grammar School, founded in 1656 by a Newport native who amassed great wealth in London, lies beyond a courtyard with almshouses on either side of substantial gate piers. A cupola on the main building houses a seventeenth-century clock. *Beaumaris House*, for boarders, is a handsome brick town house of 1724 with a pediment supported by Tuscan pillars. Thomas Brown, the seventeenth-century satirical poet, perhaps best known for his unreasoning antipathy to Dr Fell, was a scholar here, and in more recent times Sir Oliver Lodge, physicist and pioneer

in psychical research. The *Old Guildhall* (1615) is one of several timber-framed buildings which survived the fire. The red sandstone parish church is large and Victorian, well furnished with battlements and glass by Burne-Jones and Kempe. There is a chaste Greek Congregational church on the Wellington road, 1817, with the "British School" next door. The Roman Catholic church is Pugin-Tudor of brick and stone, built in 1832 by Lord Shrewsbury. Altogether, the town remains a remarkably harmonious unity, and it is to be hoped that nothing will be done to disturb or destroy such a rarity at this present time.

Newtown (5). A few miles from Wem. During the Commonwealth high churchmen of this district converted a private house into a place of worship and dedicated it to King Charles the Martyr. The present church, by E. Haycock Jnr., 1869, is tasteless though expensive. Macabre pictures depict King Charles's execution and burial. There is a stone reredos of the Last Supper. Also a wrought-iron screen.

Text in the monument:

FRANCIS ELDEST DAVGHTER TO
SIR ROBERTE NEDHAM OF SHA
VINGTON IN THE COVNTIE OF
SALLOP KNIGHT AND WIFE TO
SR ROWLAND COTTON OF AL=
KINGTON IN THE COVNTIE
KNIGHT DYED IN CHILD BED BE
ING DELIVERED OF A DAVGHTER
WHO LIKEWISE DYED ON SON
DAYE A DAYE OF RESTE BEINGE TH
23d DAYE OF NOVEMBER ANNO DOMINI
1606

Cotton monument, NORTON-IN-HALES

Norbury (10). On the southern slopes of Linley Hill and west of the Long Mynd, overlooking flatter country. The houses are grouped round the largely Victorian church (Henry Curzon, 1880 and 1892) with its broach spire sitting on an earlier tower. A rough boulder at the end of the sanctuary steps is reputed to have been used as a penance seat. This is not a specially remarkable village but there are plenty of cast-iron windows to be seen in the farm-houses and cottages.

Norton-in-Hales (6). A mainly brick village close to the Stafford-shire border in hunting country. On the village green is a great boulder called the "Bradling Stone", on which it was the custom to "bradle" or bump any man or boy found still working after noon on Shrove Tuesday. Another custom in this district was the curfew which rang at 8 from Michaelmas Day to Lady Day. The church is almost

entirely mid-Victorian with a little octagonal baptistry beside the tower, under which is the magnificent Cotton monument. This has obviously been moved from its original position, probably during the rebuilding of 1864–72, but is still a most rich and touching memorial.

Oakengates (9). A straggling industrial region which never quite manages to coalesce into anything which is recognisable as a *town*. There are ironworks and collieries all round—the coal has been worked here since Roman times—but this ragged industrial landscape never achieves the romance of that of Coalbrookdale or Madeley. At St George's is a multitude of chapels, and beside the main road is Street's church, large and low-lying. It is a massive building of rough grey stone with pink sandstone and red and yellow brick for contrast of colour and surface, still with gas

lamps. Very high and well lit by plain glass in the clerestory, this is typical of the nineteenth-century search for fresh variations on a well-used theme. It is not un-pleasant, especially when dressed for Harvest Thanksgiving.

Oldbury (12). A hill-top village near Bridgnorth with a Victorian church, but more remarkable for its fine views.

Onibury (14). A small village just north of Ludlow, where the railway crosses the main road. A pleasant collection of red brick, limestone and half-timber with the nineteenth-century prevailing. The church is small and one of the most har-monious in all Shropshire, with a plain stone exterior and rendered

ONIBURY
Interior by Detmar Blow, 1902 ▷

112

timber porch. Inside the narrow nave are solid tie-beams and white-washed walls against which Detmar Blow designed a splendid interior. The woodwork of the 1902 W. gallery is in the Art Workers' Guild style with an unusual criss-cross pattern to the screen and the Royal Arms of Edward VII in front. There are contemporary lanterns on rough-hewn oak posts in rough-hewn pews, rough hat pegs on the walls and even 1902 commandment boards on the walls. In the gallery some older panelling has been re-used. The pulpit is probably mediaeval but the memorial to Dorothy Pytt, d. 1657, is both later and cruder, though curious. *Stokesay Court* is 1889 Elizabethan by Thomas Harris, among conifers and with a pleasant lodge. The well laid out gardens are open to the public on occasion.

Oswestry (4).

> ". . . Oswestry, a pretie towne
>   full fine . . .
> It stands so trim, and is
>   maintained so cleane
> And peopled is with folke that
>   well doe meane."

So wrote Thomas Churchyard, a Shropshire poet in the seventeenth century. Near the border, Oswestry is influenced in many respects by its proximity to Wales. There is a large Welsh population and they have brought the worst of their architecture with them—red glazed brick. Its history is much more interesting than the town itself. Oswald, a Christian King of Northumbria, was killed here in battle by the pagan King Penda of Mercia in the seventh century. His body was nailed to a tree, and he was subsequently canonised and gave his name to the town. The Normans fortified it and Richard II held a parliament here in 1398. The town has seen much strife and has been ravaged by fire many times, first by King John in revenge for opposition by the townspeople in 1215. The last major fire was in 1742. Consequently, there is very little building dating from before the eighteenth century. The church of St Oswald, badly gutted by fire during the Civil War, was largely rebuilt in the seventeenth century and later on received the

attentions of Street in 1872–4. One of the better features of the interior is the large number of good memorial brasses of the seventeenth–nineteenth century. The timber-framed lych-gate, 1631, in Welsh Walls, once formed the entrance to the Grammar School. The eighteenth-century iron gates on to Church Street are also worth looking at. The best of the older buildings still standing is Llwyd Mansion, dated 1604, a black and white house with fine window tracery, now converted to shops. The Grammar School was founded in 1407, although the present buildings do not pre-date the eighteenth century. They are set on a wooded hill and include an especially fine Master's House, 1776. Canon Spooner was educated here. The Municipal Buildings are typical of late Victorian public architecture and include a small museum. The Wynnstay Hotel (T.H.), is a digni-fied late Georgian red brick building on three storeys with a deep porch and two pairs of Tuscan columns. The Ministry of Social Security is housed in a former chapel of 1830, with arched windows and a Greek Doric doorway. The former Victoria Works, 1870, now a garage, was once an iron foundry with extensive buildings behind. It forms an attractive reminder that there was once considerable industry in the town.

A few yards away an antique shop now occupies the stables of the former Raven Inn. In the interim, however, the premises had been used by a plumber and glazier and the apprentices' test windows can still be seen on the first floor. The Secondary Modern School by Richard Sheppard, 1956–8, is "one of the best recent buildings in the county" (Pevsner). Probably a fair judgment, but there is so little to compare it with. Fairholme, next door, an old people's home built in 1963, is a worthy neighbour.

Sir Walford Davies, the composer, and Wilfred Owen, perhaps the best of all the First World War poets, were both born in Oswestry. *Old Oswestry* is a good example of an Iron Age fort. *Sweeney Hall* is a freestone house of 1805 in a land-scaped park with a Commonwealth burial ground in front. Sweeney

Mountain is a nearby beauty spot with some good views. Coal was formerly mined hereabout and carried on the Shropshire Union Canal.

Oxon (8). Almost absorbed by Shrewsbury; an unremarkable main-road settlement. Church 1745 by Haycock, and pseudo-Elizabethan mental hospital, 1845.

Peplow (9). A small village near Hodnet. A pair of fine wrought-iron gates lead to *Peplow Hall*, the early eighteenth-century home of the Vic-torian millionaire philanthropist Francis Stanier, d. 1900. A con-temporary newspaper says he was very fond of birds, and had some favourite American and Japanese geese, which he fed with his own hands. Just before he died over 100 of these birds flew round his bed-room window outside (they were kept on a pool near his home), beating against the glass. They then flew over the roof, making a weird screaming noise. In his last moments the whole flock disappeared, and not one was ever seen again.

The Chapel of the Epiphany was designed by Norman Shaw in 1878 to replace the old chapel of ease. It has a delightful setting with yews and conifers in a railed-off corner of the grounds of the hall. The construction is red brick set in half-timber with very high roof and an open bellcote. Inside, a very dark wall painting in the chancel spoils what ought to be the climax of this little chapel.

Petton (8). Set amid green fields, this hamlet consists of a few houses, the church and the well-wooded Petton Park (now a school). The church is set on a knoll, closely fenced against grazing sheep. Red brick, of 1727, with dark, oak-panelled walls and box-pews facing inwards, chapel fashion, across a wide aisle. A very high Jacobean pulpit with ornate tester. Dark, but wholly peaceful, with the sun stream-ing up the aisle from the open door at the time of our visit.

Pitchford (11). The village takes its name from a bituminous well, now long dry, but is best known as the site of *Pitchford Hall*, the queen of

PITCHFORD Hall

Shropshire's black and white houses. It was built by Adam Otley, c. 1560–70, before the decimation of our forests caused brick and stone to replace such mansions. It stands on a little knoll "surrounded by well disposed grounds, diversified with an abundance of wood and a small stream flowing in front of the house" (Hulbert). It is wholly timber-framed with diagonal struts making a fine lozenge pattern and with a stone-slated roof with star-shaped brick chimneys. Built on an E-plan, it faces out across parkland, but the present main entrance faces towards the church and is approached through a fine avenue of lime trees. A great lime in the garden supports a pretty Gothic tree-house of about 1760. The church, surrounded by yews and nestling beside the Hall, seems to have been protected thus from the ministrations of the restorers. It has some Norman features, including herring-bone stonework, but is mainly Early English with a long, narrow nave, still plastered inside. There are hatchments, seventeenth-century box-pews, a Jacobean pulpit and communion rails and a nineteenth-century organ cast in the Gothic tradition. A huge wooden effigy of a knight in chain-mail probably commemorates a member of the Pitchford family, but best of all are the incised alabaster slabs of husbands and wives of the family, with some fifty of their children at their feet. These range from 1529 to 1587 and make a wonderful gallery of costume of that period.

Pontesbury (11). Dairy-farming lowlands with some associated industry and quarrying nearby on the margin of the Stiperstones upland. Pontesford Hill (1,047 ft.) dominates, with its steep slopes and windswept, tree-lined crest overlooking the gentler meadows of the Rea valley. Banks and ditches of prehistoric camps abound on the surrounding hills, where a great battle was fought in the seventh century between the kings of Mercia and Wessex. Old Pontesbury is a small town rather than a village, with a tight arrangement of buildings in the centre, the recent development preserving this compact character in contrast to the less happy building sprawl of rather earlier date. The large church was rebuilt in 1829 except for the thirteenth-century chancel, which retains its original roof of trussed beams. The curious mixture of grey limestone and red sandstone inside shows the extent of the renewal. All traces of the eighteenth century have disappeared. There is an especially fine memorial to Thomas Davies, a London merchant who died in 1674, with figures of two women and children, and a splendid sailing ship blown along by the Spirit of the Wind. In the churchyard a good classical cast iron tomb of the Rev. Hamlet Harrison, Rector of Pontesbury (First Portion), d. 1843, also another cast-iron tombstone with attached oval plaque. This was formerly a very large parish (divided into three "Portions"), as the existence of the Deanery indicates. In the late nineteenth century two rectors shared the duties at Pontesbury church but, not being entirely filled with brotherly love, one of them built St Anne's church at nearby Lea Cross and ministered from there. This is in harsh red brick with some grey marble inside, contrasting with the exposed brick but with quite an impressive chancel.

Mary Webb lived at Pontesbury for two years and at "Roseville" (now modernised) wrote one of her best-known books—*The Golden Arrow*.

Prees (5). Climb the hill to the east of the main road to the older and more interesting part of the village. There one finds a little cluster of buildings grouped round the red sandstone church. Basically it is fourteenth century with a mid-eighteenth-century tower, but the whole suffered badly from a bout of Victorian restorations. The inside is rather dark, although this helps to set off the unusual shape of the W. window. There are many monuments to the Hill family, including one to Sir John Hill, Bart., d. 1874, with basso-relievo figures. Just across the road behind a tall laurel hedge is *Prees Hall*, birthplace of General Hill, Wellington's right-hand man at Waterloo. This has a Georgian red brick façade with a pediment giving an apparent unity to a rather hotch-potch arrangement behind. The views across the lower ground to the W. are fine at sunset. Fossil collectors will find an abundance of ammonites, belemites and grypheae in the strata round about.

Preston Brockhurst (8). A village green surrounded by black and white cottages with a late seventeenth-century grey stone house overlooking all. There is no church here.

Preston Gubbals (8). Just off the main road with a church by Pountney Smith, 1866, and a much earlier tower. There is an interesting fourteenth-century monument containing the bust of a man with a cross on his breast. On the main road is *Lea Hall*, an Elizabethan brick house of 1584.

Preston upon the Weald Moors (9). Unprepossessing, flat, drained country between Newport and Oakengates, reminiscent of the Fenlands. Amid marshes and willows stands a fine eighteenth-century hospital founded in 1716 under the will of Lady Catherine Herbert, widow of the last Lord Herbert of Chirbury, as a thankoffering for her rescue in the Alps by St Bernard dogs. The red brick and limestone buildings lie around three sides of a quadrangle and are approached through an avenue of tall trees and stand behind fine eighteenth-century wrought-iron gates. At the entrance are two, later, gate lodges with giant pilasters and elongated windows. The Hall is the centre of the block, very impressive with its large arched windows and pedimented doorway. A nicely proportioned Victorian clock-tower completes the composition. The oldest part, the colonnaded wing on the left, comprises the almshouses for aged ladies "of the better class", while the opposite wing was originally for children who were trained for domestic service. They wore a little white cap and apron and short-sleeved smock such as one sees illustrated by Hogarth. The whole Hospital is in a grand yet sober tradition, making a welcome focus in this flat land. The red brick church, 1739, replaces an earlier building but, apart from the woodwork, the Georgian character has been entirely lost.

Priorslee (9). A coal and iron-working district near Oakengates. The church is 1836 with later restoration but with a good roof. *Priorslee Hall* is good early eighteenth-century brick with stone quoins, and is now the headquarters of the Telford Development Corporation.

Quatford (15). From the sharp angle here one can look up the Severn towards Bridgnorth or down towards Highley. The church commands a good vantage point from its little bluff of red sandstone exposed above the main road, surrounded by pine trees, but makes a very pretty picture by itself. It was built by Roger de Montgomery as the fulfillment of a vow made by his wife to St Mary Magdalene that she would found a church on the spot where she met her husband, after her preservation from shipwreck. The Norman chancel is in a spongy tufa but the remainder of the church is very much Victorian in flavour. A little castellated folly clings to the cliff face beyond, with conifers framing what might be the ideal "Picturesque" view. A cluster of barge-boarded and lattice-porched Victorian houses and cottages snuggles at the foot of the cliff, overlooking the river. *Quatford Castle* is an orange sandstone house, heavy with castellations, perfectly sited by John Smalman in 1830.

Quatt (15). A main-road village near Bridgnorth in the midst of rich farmlands, broken by clumps of oaks and beeches away up in the hilly country to the north-east. A row of model nineteenth-century stone and timber cottages lines the road and the red brick church is set on a hillock opposite. The sturdy tower, with its circular bell openings and finials, suggests a Georgian building and it was indeed rebuilt in 1763, but inside cool cream plaster shows off the pale pink sandstone of the mediaeval structure. The polished black marble of the Wolryche tombs gleams beside the white marble figure of Mary Wolryche, d. 1678, reclining with her lute. The carving of the Jacobean pulpit and reader's desk is in a simple style but is very fine. This is not an elaborate church but it is one to come back to and enjoy for its very simplicity and harmony. Across the lane is the double-doored Queen Anne Dower house in red brick with curious flat carving flanking the windows of the upper floor. *Dudmaston Hall* is a Queen Anne house in a wooded park with lakes and conifers. "Several walks are cut through the valley, which terminates in a beautiful prospect of the River Severn. On the east are the remains of Morf Forest, which abounds with game."

Ratlinghope (11). Pronounced "Ratchup". Narrow roads and lanes lead over the Long Mynd and up from the E. Onny River to this isolated hamlet cowering among the hills. This is almost mountain country, bleak and inhospitable in winter, but superb scenery at all times and in all weathers. The treeless top is a windswept russet brown splashed with brilliant green, like a lichen-spotted tombstone, and glowing with heather in late summer. Lower down are bracken and pine trees and the river tumbling on a stony bed. The little grey stone and slate church is pleasant, though restored, with two fonts and a door made and given by the churchwardens in 1625. All around, in the hills, are pre-historic sites; the great camp on Ratlinghope Hill is the one described by Mary Webb in *The Golden Arrow*.

Richard's Castle (Batchcott) (17). The church stands just inside the Shropshire border while the rest of the village lies in Herefordshire. The approach from Ludlow is through magnificent beech woods, at their best in spring and autumn.

The new church is an imposing building of cathedral-like propor-tions, half-buried among trees on the Ludlow side but with the tower standing up splendidly on the hill when viewed from the village. This is the best side from which to view it, with the sun to give life to the window openings and an avenue of yews up to the tower. It was built in a yellow rock-faced stone to Norman Shaw's design in 1891–2 and most of the cost was borne by Mrs Johnston Foster, a generous-hearted lady who liked things large. Shaw must certainly have pleased her with his immense tower and spacious interior, which is enormous and quite bare apart from the ingenious and beautiful tracery and the focus-ing of detail round the altar. The rectory is an apricot colour-washed brick Georgian house with pretty windows and stands on a little hill across the road. At Moor Park is a Queen Anne-style brick house in that parkland back towards Ludlow.

Rodington (9). Like Withington, a canal village, but here the Shrop-shire Union is carried over the River Roden. The picturesque canal bridge of the type so often drawn and painted by Van Gogh and Rem-brandt now stands still and derelict. This is flat country where silver birches quiver and rustle in the wind. Just a few red brick cottages and farms and a dull 1851 church.

Rowton (8). A hamlet on a little rise near High Ercall. Richard Baxter, the eminent Nonconformist divine and author of the *Saints' Everlasting Rest*, was born here in 1615. There was a mediaeval church here but the present building is almost entirely nineteenth century.

Rushbury (14). In beautiful Apedale, under the slopes of Wenlock Edge, where a twisting road creeps down Roman Bank to cross the Eaton Brook over a packhorse bridge. This is said to have been an old

The Hospital, Preston upon the Weald Moors, 1716

St Martin's

Roman station and it certainly looks as if it might have been. The school and Old Rectory make a compact group with the mainly thirteenth-century church; the inside is very plain, plastered walls and good roofs, typical Border work with wind-braces and hammer-beams in the chancel. The squat tower forms the focal point, with the 1840 Tudor–Gothic rectory hiding behind conifers, and below, the handsome timber-framed Rushbury Manor with its massive stone chimney. The school is a decent classic design of 1821 with an inscription over the door and almshouses alongside. On Stanway Manor is a farm designed in 1891 by J. Brooks. Wilderhope Manor is a charming, irregular stone house of 1586, hidden away by itself in a fold of Wenlock Edge. It was purchased by John Cadbury and given to the National Trust on condition that it be used as a Youth Hostel. On Wednesday afternoons in summer it is open to visitors, and the seventeenth-century plaster ceilings should not be missed. They are almost certainly the work of the craftsman who worked at Morville and Upton Cressett.

Lutwyche Hall has undergone several changes. It was built as a noble brick mansion in 1587 to an E-plan, on the site of an earlier stone house. The spaces between the wings were filled in during the eighteenth century and Pountney Smith was responsible for further work in 1851. The house subsequently became Wenlock Edge School and is now a hotel.

Ruyton XI Towns (8). Large mainroad village leading down to Telford's bridge over the R. Perry. One of eleven townships making the Manor of Ruyton, with a Charter dated 1301. The original mace is still in existence. All that remains of the early fourteenth-century castle, built by the Earl of Arundel, lord of the manor, is a mound of stones in the churchyard. The red sandstone church has an attractive interior despite much restoration. Norman nave and chancel with Norman windows. *Ruyton Manor* incorporates all the features of a mediaeval castle. Victorian castellated, c. 1860.

Ryton (8). A secluded spot in a gentle landscape of willows and mature trees near the valley of the Worfe. The unremarkable church has an early eighteenth-century tower and chancel, but the interior has been thoroughly restored with typical Victorian zeal. The bridge over the Worfe makes a picturesque scene.

St George's (see Oakengates).

St Martin's (4). Pretty almshouses beside the church dated 1810 on front but 1638 on E. end. A single-storey range with central pediment, of red brick with stone dressings and diamond glazing bars in wood. Good, simple architecture. The thirteenth-century church is one of the best in Shropshire. The tower (1632) is rather reminiscent of the Cotswolds in its colour and texture. The interior is rich without over-elaboration. Steps lead from the porch to a W. gallery which has been glassed in very successfully. Box-pews in dark oak and stained deal have beautifully engraved brass nameplates on the doors. The Trevor and some other pews are fitted up in red baize. The double-decker pulpit is hung with its original Georgian velvet. Hatchments, royal arms, turned communion rails. Secondary Modern School by Sir Basil Spence 1954–7: steel frame with vertical boarding infill panels. Large colliery at Ifton Heath. Canal settlement on Gobowen road has some simple terraces and blocks.

Sambrook (9). A variegated sandstone church, 1856, by Benjamin Ferrey, but not as good as his nearby St Michael's, at Chetwynd. It has a curious little weather-boarded belfry and shingled broach spire. The country here is pleasant but unremarkable.

Selattyn (4). Romantic country, very hilly and practically in Wales. Narrow lanes wind up among wooded slopes. On a hill close by is a tower built to commemorate a battle between Britons and Saxons, placed here by a clergyman in 1847. The mediaeval church has a tower of 1704 and after additions in the 1820s was restored by Hodgson Fowler in 1892. The roofs are original and very fine, too, cusped wind-braces and much elaborate carving. Dr Sacheverell, the polemical high churchman, had this living conferred on him after his trial in 1710. He made a triumphal journey by way of Oxford and Bridgnorth, accompanied sometimes by 4,000 people on horseback and as many on foot.

South-east of Selattyn and reaching almost into Oswestry is the park of *Brogyntyn* (earlier Porkington, earlier still Constable's Hall), the seat of Lord Harlech. The house is a chaste and correct classical building mostly of the early nineteenth century. The park is magnificently wooded in a picturesque landscape style, and from the long walk there is a remarkable view over the rich and highly ornamental plains of Shropshire. In the other direction is a tremendous view of the Welsh hills. There is much old timber in this park, and some excellent early nineteenth-century planting, now in its prime.

Llanforda Hall, 1½ miles S.W. of Brogyntyn, was built in 1780, but only the stables survive, as farm buildings.

Shawbury (8). A meeting place of several routes near the R. Roden but now becoming almost a small town centred on the R.A.F. station here. The pleasantest part is round the church where something of the village character remains: a black and white thatched house, some fancy plaster-work and a good Georgian red brick hotel with a garden-house. The church is late Norman, in Grinshill stone, with a fifteenth-century tower and pleasant little

Wilderhope Manor near RUSHBURY

porch. Inside are some fragments of good sixteenth-century glass, a Jacobean pulpit and eighteenth-century brass chandelier, all worth seeing. The strange carved and painted reredos was made by a local lady in 1881.

Sheinton (11). A side road from Cressage slips back over the Harley Brook and climbs the wooded slopes of the north end of Wenlock Edge. Across the Leech Meadow the Severn winds in one of its great bows before sweeping into the gorge. The church clings to the face of a steep cliff. It is mainly Victorian, S. Pountney Smith, 1854, but has a seventeenth-century bellcote with a pyramid roof. Inside is a miniature stone effigy of a gaily smiling woman holding a book under her arm, probably of the thirteenth century.

Shelve (10). On remote, windswept, desolate slopes, below the craggy

quartzite outcrops of the Stiperstones, where whinberries and bilberries grow and where waste heaps and stone buildings of now-deserted lead mines are scattered over the lonely landscape. Some of these mines were worked by the Romans and pigs of lead bearing Hadrian's stamp have been found. At Shelve stands the tiny stone church of All Saints, serving a small and scattered community. Built in 1839, with a barrel roof and refurbished (but not improved) in 1884. *Pennerley:* even more isolated and below the boulders of the Devil's Chair. There are confused and extensive mine workings and a small chapel. The decayed ruins of the mining industry of the area have blended and become part of the landscape; not so the rusting wrecks of old cars dumped there in more recent years.

Sherifhales (9). There are some good brick barns on the approach to the village and a pretty nineteenth-

century black and white lodge beside the church. The nave was added in 1661 with piers and arches plundered from the recently destroyed Lilleshall Abbey. The chancel is eighteenth century with the ceiling plastered over later. The pleasantest feature is the churchyard: some good stones well enclosed by yews.

Shifnal (12). This was once a pleasant place with black and white half-timber and Georgian, and earlier, red brick houses. The railway came and sliced through the centre and the town has never recovered. Industrialism has helped to swamp it, and it is distressing to see so much decent building subject to so much neglect. If just a fraction of the energy being put into Telford (just down the road) were diverted here Shifnal could become a decent place to live in once more. The large red sandstone church has been scraped and much restored by Gilbert Scott in 1876–9, but yet has Norman

SHIFNAL

120

SHIPTON Hall stables

and later features and some good monuments. Outside, the setting has been ruined by the thoughtless removal of all the tombstones and the completely tasteless replacement with mediocre municipal-style planting, complete with concrete paths and lamp posts. A ghastly warning of what is done in the name of "tidying up", and quite inexcusable. On the fringes and outside the town some good houses remain: *Idsall House*, good red brick William and Mary, complete with tulip motifs; Haughton Hall, 1718, cream stuccoed splendour on the Wellington road. It was while staying here that Bishop Percy discovered the old manuscript which formed the basis of his Reliques. Just across the border, in Staffordshire, is Weston Park, home of the Earls of Bradford, with a park laid out by Capability Brown.

Shipton (14). Below Wenlock Edge and beside the River Corve, a charming and very English grouping with the hall and stable range and the church beside it on a little hill. Shipton Hall is a fine Elizabethan house of c. 1587 built by Richard Lutwyche in the local grey limestone, quite unspoiled and with its star-shaped chimney stacks. The house was enlarged at the back in the mid-eighteenth century and the fine

stable wing added at the same time. The pink-washed church has a low, weather-boarded tower and a Norman nave. The interior was scraped and rather spoiled in 1905, but there is still some seventeenth-century glass and good hatchments, also an interesting painted wooden monument to Mary Mytton, d. 1640. The chancel was "re-edificed and builded of newe from the foundacion and glased at the chardges of John Lutwich youngest sonne of Richard Lutwich of Lutwich Hall in the xxxj yeare of the Gracious reigne of Queene Elizabeth 1589".

Shrawardine (8). Small village along the Severn. Only a few craggy blocks of masonry remain to mark the site of the mediaeval keep which was dismantled after a successful siege by the Roundheads in 1645. Its stones were used to repair Shrewsbury Castle. The church has a red sandstone nave and chancel with weather-boarded belfry. Nave rebuilt in 1649, chancel 1722, and the whole restored in 1893. Interior cleanly decorated; some Jacobean woodwork and eighteenth-century brass. Superb views of the Breidden Hills. The village has some thatched half-timber cottages among trees. Shrawardine Pool is a stretch of water 40 acres in extent and a haunt of wildfowl.

Shrewsbury (8).

"The towne of Shrobbesbyri standithe on a rokky hill of stone of a sadde redd earth, and Severne so girdethe in all the towne that savinge a little pece . . . it were an isle." Leland

Four hundred years have not changed the essential character of this hill-town, and the encircling Severn has ensured that the centre did not spread much beyond the limits of the old town walls. Being defended on three sides by the river there was need only to place the Norman castle in the gap to seal off the remaining approach to make the town become almost impregnable. The line of the walls is set back from the river and what the eighteenth-century maps showed as open ground has largely remained as such, with even the avenues and paths marked out at that time still in existence. Two bridges, both of classic beauty, cross the Severn into the city. The English bridge is generally accepted as being designed by John Gwynne in 1774 (he also built Magdalen Bridge at Oxford and the bridge at Atcham), and the Welsh bridge is by Carline and Tilley, 1795, replacing a mediaeval one with a gate-tower. It is still possible to follow the path along the

river bank from one bridge to the other, tracing for a mile or so the great bow of the river. Possible, too, to trace the old walls (built during the reign of Henry III, 1226–56) by the line of the streets: Town Walls, Murivance, St Chad's Terrace and Claremont Bank, all following a tighter arc but still in their original bastion shape. Many of the street names in the old town are puzzling—Murivance, already mentioned, but also Mardol, Dogpole, Shoplatch and Wyle Cop; these are of mainly mediaeval derivation, but there are the "occupation" names—Milk Street, Fish Street, Butcher Row, and the former Baker Street, Shoe-makers' Row and Kiln Lane. Later developments are reflected in such names as Belmont, Claremont and Crescent Lane. Naturally enough, in a town as old as this, there is a marked tendency for buildings to relate in age to the antiquity of the street names and so the oldest

◁ ▽ Sʜʀᴇᴡsʙᴜʀʏ station

cluster together in the very heart of the town and close to the castle

Although Shrewsbury is now surrounded on all sides by suburban and industrial development, no matter which of the nine major routes one takes into the town one cannot help but be aware of the hilly centre set round with water and topped with the spires and towers of its many churches. Entering the town is perhaps less exciting, even something of a disappointment, for there are no wide main streets, no imposing market places or tree-lined squares. The pattern is hard to detect since it is the result of growth rather than planning and it is only slowly that the town reveals herself. First, one must explore on foot; this is certainly no place for cars, scarcely even for horse-drawn traffic one would have thought, judging by the steepness of some of the hills. Fortunately, all is compact and whichever of the narrow and sharply-turning streets one takes one is soon back in sight of the ever-present river and its bridges, from which to take one's bearings.

Perhaps the most striking thing about Shrewsbury is the abundance of half-timbered houses, and its claim to be "England's finest Tudor town" has much justification. These are not merely preserved buildings, though; they are in use as shops, banks and hotels and avoid any sense of preciousness or artificiality about the place. This is a thriving business, market and industrial centre for the border country, and sentiment has not been allowed to override commonsense in the matter of preserving the past. This is not to say that all is perfect in the way in which new building has been placed alongside the old, yet one is grateful that so much is still there. As in almost any town of this size, it is the traffic which detracts from the pleasures of exploring the town, but there are plenty of little alleys and passages which are only accessible on foot. Perhaps the very heart of Shrewsbury lies in the narrow lanes weaving in and out on different levels round St Alkmund's and St Julian's where they stand within a stone's throw of each other on the hill. All round are timber-framed and stuccoed houses and

cottages and the covered Bear Steps leading up to St Alkmund's and the seventeenth-century brick Kingston House. "Square" and "Place" create a false impression as names of these small and irregularly-shaped spaces with their occasional tree, rather grand eighteenth-century titles for a townscape which is entirely mediaeval in character. St Alkmund's slender Perpendicular spire points delicately upwards for almost 200 feet to make one of the key points on the Shrewsbury skyline. The

tower and spire are all that remain of the old church, which was pulled down as a result of the scare over St Chad's. The new building was built by Messrs Carline and Tilley, local architects and builders, who were also responsible for the Welsh bridge. It was completed in 1795 in Strawberry Hill Gothic style, but between 1895 and 1900 much money was spent in a foolish attempt to make the interior look Perpendicular, and much of the cast iron tracery was removed. The nave is aisleless

The English Bridge, SHREWSBURY

and the most striking feature is Francis Eginton's transparency, "Faith", in the east window. It is a copy after a painting by Guido Reni and, while rare and highly skilful, it will not appeal to everyone. St Julian's also has an old tower with a later nave, late Norman with Perpendicular work above, but this is a much older church, possibly the oldest foundation in the town. It was originally St Juliana's but usage has "changed" the dedication. The parish registers here go back in unbroken line to 26 September 1559. The church was rebuilt in 1750 by T. F. Pritchard, another local architect, at a cost of £1,440. As with St Alkmund's, it was thought necessary to interfere with, and spoil, a good design during the nineteenth century and thus in 1846 the exterior was "beautified". The inside is fortunately not spoiled and worth seeing for the way in which the earlier structure has been incorporated with the new so successfully. Grope Lane, well known for its overhanging half-timbered houses which almost meet overhead, leads from this self-contained area to St Mary's Street. Here is the cathedral-like St Mary's church, whose spire is companion to that of St Alkmund's in any distant prospect of the town and one of the tallest in England. The building is of well-weathered pink sandstone and though scraped inside it is of such a size and so fine in its proportions and detailing that such insensibility may be overlooked, if not forgiven. Note especially the beautiful south porch and its doors made up from the old rood screen. Once inside, it is the glass which makes the first impact; it is good, the best in the whole of Shropshire, although scarcely any of it was, in fact, made for St Mary's. The greatest splendour is to be seen in the E. window in a Tree of Jesse made in the fourteenth century, probably for the Franciscan church, but moved to St Chad's and finally, in 1792, to St Mary's. Most of the remainder of the glass is continental, fifteenth and sixteenth century, that

◁ St. Alkmund's, SHREWSBURY

in N. aisle is from Trèves and better than the rest. But apart from the glass, the church can be enjoyed as a whole and has more unity than most. The sturdy Norman work in the chancel and transepts blossoms superbly in the capitals of the nave arcades—delicately carved as part of the complex pier arrangement, inviting comparison with a cathedral church.

Not far away is black and white Butcher Row, narrow and over-topped by the long range of Grey-hound Chambers, jutting further forward on each of its three storeys and matched by its counterpart, the Abbot's House, opposite. Built in the mid 1400s, this is a fine house, less ambitious than the mansions of the High Street, but finely carved and with what are probably the ori-ginal arches to the shop front. It seems likely that this was not the Abbot's house at all but simply that of a butcher (a powerful and wealthy trade in mediaeval times), hence the open-fronted ground floor. In the High Street are two of the best-known black and white buildings in the town: Ireland's Mansion and Owen's Mansion, built c. 1575 and 1592 respectively as a mark of success in the wool trade, upon which so much of the town's pros-perity depended at that time. Had it not been for wool, not only would the East Anglian and Cotswold churches and houses have been less magnificent, but neither would there have been such splendid timber building in the Border counties. High Street widens out here to form the Square, once a civic, commercial and cultural centre with Sir Robert Smirke's classic Shire Hall, 1836, Haycock's Music Hall, 1840, and best of all, in the centre, Walter Hancock's Old Market Hall, 1596. This is a plain but dignified stone building set up on columns and not without affinities with the old Shrewsbury School building. Of Hancock (see also Much Wenlock), Sir Francis Newport said "You cannot match the man in these parts (with any of that occupacon) neyther in scyence and judgement of work-manship, nor in playnes and honestye to deal with all". It is worth bearing in mind that this Market Hall is almost exactly contemporary with Owen's Mansion, yet the classic elements and plan make this essen-tially Jacobean as compared with the traditional Tudor timber house. Worth noting, too, that it was a public building setting the highest standard rather than settling for a lukewarm conservatism. Standing with his back to the Market Hall is Marochetti's statue of Robert, Lord

Milk Street leading to Belmont, SHREWSBURY

Clive, who on his return from India became M.P. for Shrewsbury from 1761 until his death in 1774. High Street is joined by Dogpole to drop down steeply to English Bridge by way of Wyle Cop and lined almost exclusively with half-timber on either side. There is a great deal of carving to the house fronts here, above shop level; the best is on Henry Tudor House, where Henry VII stayed in 1485 on his way to the battle of Bosworth. (Princess Mary Tudor, later Queen Mary, stayed at a house a few yards away in 1525.) Adjoining Tudor House is the Lion Hotel, with a pleasantly varied façade stepped down the hill and with parts dating from the fifteenth century. Robert Lawrence, an enterprising eighteenth-century landlord of the Lion, was largely responsible for routing the Holyhead road through the town and made sure that his hotel was modernised accordingly. The splendid ballroom has its original plasterwork ceiling and gallery, reputedly by Robert Adam, c. 1777, and a more than fit setting for the dances and balls which it must have seen during the Georgian era. "In the language of the gentry many miles round the Wrekin", wrote Macaulay, "to go to Shrewsbury was to go to town. The provincial wits and beauties imitated, as well as they could, the fashions of St James's Park in the walkes along the side of the Severn." Mrs Siddons appeared at the theatre here, and later on Paganini played and Jenny Lind sang in the ballroom of the Lion, a musical tradition which has been revived recently in the series of winter concerts each year.

The eighteenth century was a time when Shrewsbury prospered. As a consequence it has many good buildings of that date yet without any of the grander planning schemes which changed the face of so many towns. At the turn of the century there was the dignified and gracious Judge's Lodgings in trim red brick with white-painted sashes and pediment over the door, and Richard Newport,

◁ St. Chad's SHREWSBURY, 1790–92

newly created Earl of Bradford, was anxious to do justice to himself in his new house in Dogpole. The new Earl had a good eye for a commanding site and in order to dominate Dogpole, where it takes a turn and also enjoy fine views over the river, he moved the existing house to Castle Street and re-erected it there, where it is now known as Castle Gates House. His new house stands with authority over its humbler neighbours, red brick, stone quoins, hipped roof and all, the very picture of a Queen Anne house and serving now as the Guildhall. Similar in style, but a little later, is Dr Thomas Bowdler's School in Beeches Lane, discreet red brick of 1724 and very charming. It is scarcely an accident that one of the best late eighteenth-century houses in the town was the home of one of its most influential citizens: Sir William Pulteney, millionaire Member of Parliament for Shrewsbury and later Earl of Bath. On being elected, he decided to live in the Castle and brought his protegé Thomas Telford "to superintend a thorough renovation of the building" in 1786. This he did and added Laura's Tower, 1790, on the mound overlooking the river. Telford was also concerned with the building of Shrewsbury Gaol and as a result of his discussions with Howard the reformer, Haycock's earlier designs were modified. The most telling occurrence for Telford was when, after being consulted on the state of the roof of St Chad's church, he reported that the tower was "in a parlous state and likely to collapse", which it promptly did three days later, to the chagrin of the vestry and the enhancement of Telford's professional reputation. The stately new St Chad's was built in 1792 on the hill overlooking the Quarry, a fine open space which had been laid out and planted with an avenue of lime trees. It enjoys one of the very best sites in the whole of the county. The architect was George Steuart, designer of Attingham just a few years before, and he chose Grinshill stone for his church also. The plan is based on two intersecting circles, the smaller making an entrance hall with a splendid staircase curling round the walls and leading to the gallery of the larger,

St. Alkmund's, SHREWSBURY. East window by Francis Eginton, 1795

circular nave. This makes a fine inspiring space but it is ruined by tawdry copper fittings and crude stained glass. Completing the composition at the W. end is a square tower with a neat portico and vestries, the second stage is octagonal and is completed with a circular stage with detached columns and a dome. Opinions on this church have ranged from Southey's "preposterous structure" and Torrington's "as ugly as improper" to Mr Whiffen's "one of the most boldly conceived buildings of the whole Georgian epoch" and Prof. Pevsner's "original and distinguished design". Whatever one's personal feelings (and the writer feels that the interior has been spoiled with insensitive furnishings and glass), the tower makes a beautiful punctuation on the skyline from almost any part of the town.

Where Belmont was the fashionable new street of the beginning of the eighteenth century, a hundred years later Claremont was in vogue and that stretch of Town Walls known as the Crescent, the very names redolent of that era. The

127

best here are Claremont Buildings in ashlar by Carline and Tilley (a good firm who were active at this time both in Shrewsbury and the county), the Crescent, and Haycock's Allatt's School. The classic style is well displayed too, in his Royal Infirmary, 1826–30, with its vigorous and well-proportioned Doric façade. Unfortunately, the riverward-facing portions are less handsome and do little to improve that view of the town. The same is true of the Tudor railway station, 1903–4, which is built over the river and replaces an earlier but similar building of 1848. It stands beside, and spoils the view of, the castle, and also that view out of and into the town. In short, it usurps the rights and visual function of the castle and no amount of "period dress" can excuse this fact. Across the road from the castle gate, in the former Shrewsbury School building, is the Library and Art Gallery with an extremely good collection of books, manuscripts and prints relating to Shrewsbury and the county. The dark stone building is L-shaped with a tower at the angle, the 1590 range fronting the road and the gable of the 1630 addition stretching back. The school was founded by Edward VI in 1552, and moved to its present building across the river from St Chad's in 1882, where it occupies earlier buildings considerably altered and extended by Blomfield. In front of the old building is a statue of Charles Darwin, author of the *Origin of the Species*, who was born at Shrewsbury and educated there. His actual birthplace was at the Mount, in Frankwell, over the Welsh bridge.

Still within the town, bounded by the river, there are several more churches. The Roman Catholic Cathedral by E. Welby Pugin is an unstartling early Decorated building of 1856 without a tower. St Michael's is yellow brick classical by Carline, 1830, with a good tower. Also worth noting are the former Methodist church, 1834, Town Walls, and Unitarian, 1840, High Street.

Outside the natural boundary formed by the river is the inevitable spread and sprawl of the nineteenth and twentieth centuries, interspersed with a few relieving features. The most ancient of these is Holy Cross,

the Abbey church, founded by Roger de Montgomery about 1080 but now isolated and bereft of its monastic buildings, lonely amid the traffic. This large, pink sandstone church has been greatly, and not gently, restored, and the chancel is wholly by J. L. Pearson, 1887, in E.E. style. The nave is still massively Norman with short stubby pillars and there was once a gallery above. In Prof. Pevsner's words, "The restoration of 1862 did untold aesthetic damage to the whole", yet the extremely fine W. window was spared. St George's, Frankwell, is by Haycock, 1832, in lancet style. Close by the Abbey is Abbey House, 1725, red brick, a fine house with particularly good gates. In Coleham, near English Bridge, was the iron foundry of William Hazeldine, associate of Telford and maker of the ironwork for the Menai Bridge (see Upton Magna). He is buried in St Chad's. Off Abbey Foregate is Whitehall, a good Jacobean house built on a square plan in 1578–82 with red sandstone from the abbey and having a separate gatehouse. On the London road, and quite unmistakable, is Lord Hill's Column, the largest Doric column in the world. Based on a design by Haycock, it was completed in 1816, work having started only a few months after Waterloo. (For General Lord Hill see Hadnall and Prees.) At the Column now is the new Shire Hall and County Council building, glass and concrete, with sufficient humility not to dwarf the Column itself. It is much bolder, and therefore more successful, than the new General Market in the town centre. Beyond the railway station is what was originally the warehouse of the Shropshire Union Canal Co., built in 1835 and designed by Fallows and Hart of Birmingham. A great Greek portico with iron and glass behind. A short walk away is Spring Gardens where stands Benyon, Bage & Marshall's Flax Mill, designed in 1796 by Charles Bage and the first multi-storey iron-framed building in the world. It is now the premises of Messrs William Jones, Maltsters.

Of the more recent buildings in the town centre there is little to be said apart from one honourable exception: Lloyd's Bank on Pride

Hill. This was designed by Sir Percy Thomas & Son, 1968, as an uncompromisingly modern structure which is yet sympathetic to its surroundings.

Sibdon Carwood (14). This romantic-sounding village lies remote and inaccessible yet quite close to Craven Arms. The original church was built c. 1180 but was rebuilt in 1756 and suffered the customary attention of the nineteenth century. It now has a polygonal apse and gargoyles. Superbly well kept, it stands beyond close-mown lawns and clipped yews with its gleaming weathercock winking at *Sibdon Castle*, an early seventeenth-century house castellated in 1756.

Sidbury (15). In very attractive country south-west of Bridgnorth, where the level of the ground changes suddenly and often and has scattered woods. Down a path overhung with damson trees is the little Norman church. It was entirely renewed in the nineteenth century and again after a fire in 1912, but the well-cared-for interior is simple and pleasant. In the N. chapel are two very fine early eighteenth-century monuments to the Cresswells.

Silvington (14). Remote in a small valley on the northern slopes of Titterstone Clee. Small farms dot the landscape. The stone church has a good Norman S. doorway and arch at the base of the tower with seventeenth-century panelling in the chancel. A fine wall monument, adorned with flowers and two garlanded skulls, commemorates Edward Mytton, a former lord of the manor. A moated stone manor house, with fourteenth-century lancet windows at one end, stands close to the church.

Smethcott (or Smethcote) (11). A very remote spot on the extreme tip of the Long Mynd before it drops down into the green and fertile valley. On the top it is bleak and bare with only little folds or hollows to sustain this and the nearby hamlets of Picklescott and Walk Mills. A barren but beautiful spot with its waterfall and now almost totally Victorian church. For a

story touching on the remoteness of this district, see Woolstaston.

Snailbeach (10). A strange and beautiful landscape in the shadow of the Stiperstones and the Devil's Chair. This was once a thriving lead mining district with a little mineral railway down to Minsterley. All that remains now are ruined houses and cracked and crumbling chimneys, overgrown rails and a little loco shed. The shafts here still stretch dangerously under the hill, dark and mysterious in a quiet and forgotten place. The spoil heaps are quite stunning in their complexity of folds and blinding white with crystals of barytes, or "brightus", as they call it here.

Stanton Lacy (14). A pretty village at the southern end of Corvedale, reached from the main road by a little bridge. Warm red brick and black and white cottages and pink-washed plaster and white paint are the building colours here, with the pinky-grey sandstone church in the centre, deep set amid yews and hollies and conifers. Snowdrops cover the ground in spring while rooks wheel above. The church contains a good deal of Saxon work and it still keeps the peculiar high and narrow proportions of a Saxon building. The bulk of the work is Norman, though, with a fourteenth-century chancel and tower. The interior has been over-restored, as usual. There is a charmingly naïve plaque with cherubs and arms, to John Thynne, d. 1717.

Stanton Long (14). On the eastern hillslopes of the green and luxuriant Corvedale, with many notable brick and timber barns in the village. The

church door is probably the original from the thirteenth century but otherwise the church is over-restored. In the course of that work a good black and white roof with quatrefoil panels was uncovered, so all was not lost. A pretty winding road climbs up towards Ditton Priors and makes an especially beautiful walk.

Stanton-upon-Hine Heath (8). Flat meadows flank the winding R. Roden with the rising ground of Hine Heath to the north. This place has been little touched by modern development in spite of Shawbury airfield not far away across the fields. A little road leads to the village from Moreton Corbet, over two narrow, hump-backed bridges. The spacious Norman church looks well across the fields. Mary Webb lived here before her marriage.

Stanwardine (see Weston Lullingfields).

Stapleton (11). A red brick village with a red sandstone church which is both curious and, perhaps, unique in having two distinct storeys. It was originally Norman, c. 1200, and consisted of a church with an undercroft below. When rebuilding took place in 1786 the two were thrown into one, thus accounting for the discrepancy in wall thicknesses and the double row of windows. When the church was restored in 1867 the walls were scraped and a great deal of heavy detail was added, spoiling the whole effect. The blue and gilt wooden candlesticks stand 6 feet high and are good German pieces of about 1500. The *Moat Farm*, one mile south, is a good half-timbered house on a stone plinth and surrounded by a moat.

Stirchley (12). A small cluster of houses on the edge of a former mining area now finds itself engulfed in the Telford new town. The tiny church suggests a curious cross between church and chapel: the dimly-lit Norman chancel with its

◁ Stokesay Castle
   Gate House carving
      above Church and Castle ▷
      below Gate House

splendidly carved chancel arch pure C. of E., but the grey-painted and very high wooden gallery (1838) essentially chapel style. The nave is eighteenth century with the original box-pews and dignified double-decker pulpit all lit by clear glass. Unusual and refreshingly unspoiled.

Stockton (12). A church, eighteenth-century red brick rectory and a pretty white house with a Regency iron porch comprise this hamlet on the edge of Apley Park. The red sandstone church was so severely restored in the last century as to be scarcely recognisable as a mediaeval building. The pulpit is Jacobean. *Apley Park* is an ostentatious early nineteenth-century Gothic mansion in Grinshill stone added to the original, dignified Georgian house. At *Norton*, between here and Sutton Maddock, are the remnants of the village green with black and white half-timber, genuine and imitation. The village school is most unusual; easily taken for a church, it has a bell-tower with steep-pitched roof and a finely patterned slate roof. Two doors admit the different sexes.

Stoke St Milborough (14). The best approach is down the steep hill from Brown Clee Hill (1,600 ft.) and Abdon Burf (1,790 ft.), which tower above the road from Ludlow, "scarred with quarries, coloured with gorse and commanding a wide landscape".

From the summits you may see "over the fruitful plains of Shropshire, pleasingly varied with woody hills, and lovely vales, dotted with the humble cottage of the labourer, and the mansion of the opulent, whilst the Cambrian Hills, which rear their lofty heights in wild grandeur towards the west, give an additional charm to the enchanting scene". As you enter the village the church lies hidden behind a splendid row of chestnuts with the gate beneath and a plain early nineteenth-century stone vicarage alongside. Many springs and brooks issue from the hill slopes and one near the church is known as St Milburga's well, after the Saxon saint who fell

fainting from her horse, pursued for two days and nights by blood-hounds. Her memory is perpetuated in the dedication of the mediaeval church which has been a good deal rebuilt but with some feeling for harmony. The result is a spacious and light building with a massive yet elaborate roof and a charming timber-framed porch. In the chancel are some good memorials, and there are royal arms and a fluted thirteenth-century font. Outside, more memorial tablets climb all over the E. wall of the chancel. A few yards down the hill is a good stone-built National School, 1856, and *Moor Farm*, in half-timber.

Stoke upon Tern (6). The village stands amid meadows and corn-fields along the R. Tern. The large and handsome red sandstone Victorian church has a square, battlemented tower with a polygonal stair turret at one corner. Good alabaster effigies of Sir Reginald Corbet and his wife recline on a big tomb-chest in the chapel. The screen displays a very pleasant use of colour: the red and gilt create an illusion of green stained wood. Some early Kempe glass in the E. window is so weathered that it almost looks mediaeval. Outside, by the E. end, are some exceptionally fine early nineteenth-century tombstones. Across the river from the church stands the black and white haunted manor house of *Petsey*.

Stokesay (14). Celebrated for its castle, which, together with "The Feathers" in Ludlow, must be the most photographed place in the whole of Shropshire. And deservedly so, for this is a very beautiful spot where wooded hills form a background to the irresistibly pretty stone and half-timber gatehouse with the mediaeval stone buildings behind. The castle, really a fortified manor house, was built in about 1280 by Laurence de Ludlow with a stone hall flanked by two towers and a solar, or living range, all surrounded by a moat. Since the castle surrendered during the Civil War, it escaped undamaged, and so is well worth visiting as a beautifully preserved mediaeval house, and also for its extremely rich Elizabethan

panelling and fireplace. It is open all the year round, except Tuesdays. The church of St John Baptist fared less well at Cromwell's hands and was largely rebuilt and refurnished as a consequence. This is not entirely a loss, though, since it has resulted in our being able to see an almost perfect example of that very rare thing, a Commonwealth church. There are box-pews, including a double-canopied one, a pulpit with tester and a gallery with spindle-turning and carved panels. On the walls are biblical texts with a plastered ceiling above.

Stottesdon (15). An ancient pre-Conquest manor known as Conde-tret. In the Domesday Book its church is mentioned as possessing revenue worth 20s. per annum! Steep-banked lanes wind over sharp hills and along leafy lanes to Cleobury Mortimer. Stottesdon is secluded, looking down on the Rea Brook a mile away, far from any main road. The church is one of the most interesting in the area, both for its fourteenth-century work and also for its carving. The nave arcade is splendid with five Norman arches on capitals carved with foliage followed by Decorated work of about 1330 (further Dec. work in 1868). The fine windows at the E. end and canopied priests' seats in the chancel also date from about the same period. Some fragments of contemporary stained glass remain. Inside the tower, over the former W. doorway, is an early tympanum and lintel with carved figures of animals. The twelfth-century font is the finest in Shropshire, carved with interlace patterns, beasts, a human figure and leaf motifs. The pulpit is Jacobean and the screen Arts and Crafts Gothic of 1901. The richness of the details of this church outweigh the tactless treatment of the rest of the structure by the Victorians and others. A Wesleyan chapel of 1849 with Gothic iron windows. At *Prescott* the tiny stone bridge over the stream is reputed to be of Roman origin.

Stow (16). A tiny hamlet lying almost hidden in a secluded valley on the side of Stow Hill (1,391 ft.) overlooking the Teme valley and

The font, STOTTESDON

the border hills. Small church nestling under a grove of fir trees. Basically thirteenth century but, apart from a fine seventeenth-century black and white roof, there is little of the original to be seen. Nineteenth-century glass and Art Nouveau mosaics. Well worth visiting for its fine situation.

Sutton (8). A ruined chancel in a farmyard is all that remains of the church of St John. A farm, a cottage and a mill make up Sutton spa, whose water is said to resemble that of Leamington.

Sutton Maddock (12). A main-road village above the Severn valley near Coalport. The uninspired church of

1888 is saved by a fine red sandstone tower dated 1579 capped with battlements and pinnacles.

Sychtyn (4). A bleak, mountainous spot on the Welsh border, not far from Oswestry. There are worked-out limestone quarries and two chapels but no church.

Tasley (12). A mere hamlet set on a hill to the north of the Bridgnorth–Much Wenlock road with extensive views of the surrounding country. The church is uninspired architecturally and is built of a resistant yellow brick which has defied the maturing effects of the weather for more than a century. The design was by Josiah Griffith (1840) in the

Early Pointed style. The interior is plain with 1840 poppy-head pew-ends, a high Jacobean pulpit and reading desk and fifteenth-century screen and font. The pale blue-grey of the chancel walls makes a pretty contrast with the text boards.

Telford (12). The "New Town" which incorporates Dawley, Madeley, Ironbridge and Coalbrookdale and all that area between Wellington–Oakengates to the north and the R. Severn to the south. For details, see under individual place-names.

Tibberton-cum-Cherrington (9).

Cherrington. A place of flattish meadows and model Victorian brick cottages. *Cherrington Manor*, traditionally the "House that Jack Built", is a rambling black and white half-timbered house of 1635.
Tibberton, separated from its twin by half a mile, has more red brick cottages with a scattering of thatch. The red sandstone church standing on a slope is early Victorian Gothic, 1842, with a battlemented tower. It replaces an earlier church with a squat bell turret with pyramid cap in true border style. The brick factory in the centre of the village was formerly a paper mill—the last in Shropshire, closed down in 1912. Harper Adams Agricultural College lies in this parish—red brick municipal-style, and no beauty.

Tilstock (5). A red brick village in the flattish N. Shropshire landscape. The church (1835) is in the same material and has a tall elongated steeple in the eighteenth-century tradition. The glazing bars are good, in cast iron like those at Adderley and St Alkmund's, Shrewsbury. The inside is delightful: pale green walls with cast-iron gallery rails in green, blue, grey and gold; a Gothic organ-case in grey and gold. Treacly yellow-varnished pine pews were glowing in afternoon sunlight when we were there and the whole church was filled with the colour and scents of fruits and flowers for the Harvest Home. *Alkington Hall*, on

TILSTOCK Church

Counterweighted bridge ▷
on the Shropshire Union
near TILSTOCK

Tong Church

the back road to Whitchurch, is a
farmhouse and all that remains of an
Elizabethan brick mansion of 1592.
It makes a fine silhouette against
the sky with its stepped and pin-
nacled gables. Close by is a canal
bridge which would not have appeared strange to Van Gogh.
Operated by a counterweight it
allows passage to the boats on a
beautiful stretch of the Welsh section
of the Shropshire Union Canal.

Tong (12). Tong church, "the village
Westminster Abbey of all the Vernons" (Burritt), is a large and
splendid Perpendicular building. It
has been carefully treated but was
rather too much restored at the end
of the last century, when the floors

◁ The monuments, TONG

were covered throughout with hard,
shiny red tiles, instead of the old
brick and stone, although a few of
the original tiles have been relaid.
All of those windows not stained
were filled with greenish tinted
glass. The walls have been scraped
of their wash and decoration except
in the Golden Chapel, where remains
of the gilding and stencilling survive.
The church was almost entirely rebuilt
in 1410 after Lady Elizabeth Pembruge founded a chantry college here
for "a warden and four priests, two
clerks and thirteen poor people".
On the Feast of John the Baptist
each year Lady Elizabeth is commemorated by a chaplet of roses laid
on the tomb she shares with her
husband, Sir Fulke de Pembruge.
Most of the other fine effigies are of
the Vernon family, of various dates
from 1451 to 1550. The "Golden
Chapel", built in 1515 by Sir Henry

Vernon, is a small but exquisite
chantry with a fan-vaulted stone
ceiling on which traces of gilding
still remain. In the church are fine
brasses and parclose screens with
remains of painting. Dickens said
he had this church in mind when he
brought Little Nell and her father
to stay in a church. The porch
where they rested still has a board
giving a schedule of occasions when
the Great Bell is to be rung. In 1760
George Durant bought Tong Castle
and commissioned Capability Brown
to remodel the house in a highly
exotic Moorish-Gothic style, and
this was indeed his masterpeice.
Now, sadly, demolished, it no
longer dominates the landscape
beyond the long, winding lake, but
many of the other follies and
fancies remain, including the Egyp-
tian aviary. It has been said that
"What the Dashwoods were to

West Wycombe, the Durants were to Tong"! Certainly their influence ranged very wide in the neighbourhood and their family motto *Beati qui Durant* ("Blessed are those who endure"), or, with its play on their name, "Blessed are the Durants", seems peculiarly apt. Elihu Burritt was surely one of the first American tourists to visit Tong; in 1868 he wrote, "He took us to his school, which was a great stone martin-box standing on 4 posts with a stairway at one end ascending to the door. The room was full of children, rural, ruddy and happy as birds. . . ."

Trefonen (7). A scattered hamlet four miles west of Oswestry, where the land rises into bolder hills. There is a grey stone church built in 1821 for the Welsh-speaking population,

also a Welsh Calvinistic Methodist chapel.

Tuck Hill (15). A mere handful of houses and farms and a totally unremarkable church by St Aubyn (1869). Nevertheless, this is a spot which should on no account be missed; it is a perfect example of how an uninspiring building takes on a sort of grandeur when it forms a part of a perfect setting. The approach is highly dramatic, along a grassy path under massive beeches and Spanish chestnuts, opening suddenly into a clearing with the little church completely surrounded by trees and hidden from the outside world.

Tugford (14). A stream gurgles down the hill from Abdon with the steep

slopes of Brown Clee behind, and this is the best approach to the village. It is sheltered in a deep fold of the hill, amid orchards, stone-gabled farms and not one inharmonious house to be seen. The simple Norman church still keeps its magnificent doorway and the thirteenth-century tower was battlemented in 1720. Just inside are two sheila-na-gigs (fertility figures), hiding in the shadows. Clear glass lets in light on to the old box-pews and small gallery but the effect is spoiled by brown and cream painted walls like a dingy school corridor. At *Earnstrey*, towards Ditton Priors, is a half-timbered manor house with mature yew trees.

Uffington and **Haughmond** (8). Uffington Village lies squeezed be-

TUGFORD inside

tween the Shropshire Union Canal and the River Severn at the foot of the wooded slopes of Haughmond Hill. The village is quiet and unremarkable with a Victorian church by S. Pountney Smith, 1856. There are some colourful roundels of German and Netherlandish glass in the windows. About a mile to the east, set against the slopes of "yon bosky hill", are the ruins of Haughmond Abbey. The delight of Haughmond is its unexpectedness; what ought to be an abbey appears to be a mansion, complete with Elizabethan gateway. In fact, of course, the buildings were secularised after the Dissolution and massive Elizabethan fireplaces were installed to mitigate the rigours of life in the former monastic quarters. The range which greets one was once the infirmary. On the eastern side

the abbey buildings were set on foundations hewn out of the solid rock of the hillside and it is here that the chapter house still stands complete. The façade is magnificent, with three grand Norman arches with statues between the pillars, and inside, a thirteenth-century figure of the Virgin and Child. Across a 60-acre lake once stood *Sundorne Castle*, by James Wyatt. Now all that remains are the castellated red brick gatehouse and chapel, the latter sadly relegated to use as a barn.

Uppington (11). A very mellow village on the western margins of the Wrekin, which glowers menacingly in the stormy light of a winter afternoon. The church is largely Victorian but there is a Norman window and

what seems to be a Saxon tympanum with a dragon over a door in the N. wall. The timber porch was built by Frances Boycott in 1678. He and his brother were granted arms by Charles II for loyalty to Charles I and for supplying munitions in 1663. A Roman altar in the N. wall was dug up in the churchyard close by. The *Tudor House* is a half-timbered house of pleasing proportions and with a richly carved porch.

Upton Cresset (12). The only approach is by a twisting, winding road down a hill, across a ford and up a steep, narrow and ultimately unmetalled road. Both the church and hall lie revealed at last in a splendid setting among trees across a valley. The little Norman church with its timber-framed turret lies half hidden

TUGFORD outside

UPTON CRESSET Gate house

behind trees, and the wooden porch conceals a good Norman doorway. The brass to Robert Cressett, 1640, has been removed to Monkhopton for safe keeping; it is signed Fr. Grigs who, as Pevsner points out, is the artist of another excellent monument at Framlingham, Suffolk. What is now a farm was once *Upton Hall*, home of the Cresset family, a remarkable Tudor brick house of c. 1540 with a gatehouse dated 1580. This now stands in an orchard, its polygonal turrets proudly against the sky. A fine relationship of buildings now emerges from the former ruin and the recent work can be seen as restoration, not only of the hall, but of excellent landscape.

Upton Magna (8). Stiuated below the stony outcrop of Haughmond Hill with good views of the majestic Wrekin to the west. Upton Magna is an unpretentious village with several

good black and white houses close to the church, one with cruck construction and another with bold diagonal strutting. The church is one of the few English churches dedicated to St Lucy and, while originally Norman, was restored and added to by G. E. Street in 1856. The result is remarkably satisfying here; Street added a N. aisle and thus made the interior very airy and spacious. The detail is rich but not obtrusive—there is a great deal of painting, including the pulpit, chancel roof beams and the organ case. Even the pretty candle brackets remain. A very fine monument to W. Barker, d. 1644, painted and in excellent condition. Outside, the W. tower is a good example of strong and sturdy Perp. work with diagonal buttresses, well weathered now but of great dignity. At Upton Forge, by the bridge over the Tern, stood the iron works where the links were forged for Telford's Menai Bridge.

Waters Upton or **Upton Parva** (9). Originally Walter's Upton, after an early Lord of the Manor, Walter Fitz-John. By-passed by the Wellington–Market Drayton road and close to the River Tern. The pink sandstone church is by G. E. Street, 1865, but there is a reference to an earlier building of 1715.

Wellington (9). This is the second largest town in Shropshire and it is a busy and progressive place. Sited at the foot of the Wrekin, and straddling the Roman Watling Street, which later became the Holyhead road (A.5), it has always been close to an important routeway. This was especially true during the era of the mail coach, and the construction of the Shropshire Union Canal and the main line railway system contributed to its importance in the eighteenth and nineteenth-centuries. The proximity of the iron and coal industries, which flourished with such distinction during that period, played no small part in the town's prosperity. Almost throughout the Civil War the town was a Royalist stronghold and Charles I gathered his entire forces here before marching off to Shrewsbury. Today, the town's industries include the manufacture of vehicle wheels, agricultural equipment, sugar beet pulp, furniture, toys and brewing; the sixteenth-century bell-founding trade has vanished, as have the nineteenth-century nailworks and glass furnaces. Strangely, there are fewer really old buildings than one would expect in such a long-established town. Most of the civic buildings belong to this century and are not unpleasing. Among the rest is a sprinkling of black and white (old and new), Shropshire-brick Georgian, and, of course, the restrained and dignified stone of All Saints' church contrasting with the more modest buff brick Christ Church. The town is torn in two by a deep railway cutting and station which run right through the centre. This must prove a nightmare to the planning authorities if they are to attempt to preserve something of the coherence of the area in the neighbourhood of the Square. This is all alleys and passages, narrow streets twisting and winding with dramatic glimpses and views of good façades and shop fronts—all good townscape. Ominously, the High Street no longer feels important and the new shopping area is being developed *outside* the close network of the existing hub of the town. The Police Headquarters represents the first stage of the new Civic Centre. Twice a week the town bursts into colour and animation with its street markets. All Saints' church is a building of great beauty, designed by George Steuart and built in 1790. The W. front is richly textured and smoke blackened, no doubt as a consequence of the railway which runs alongside but is mercifully hidden in its cutting. The churchyard has been stripped of its iron and stone tombs and is crying out for some judicious tree planting to clothe the present nakedness. The inside has been re-pewed, and largely spoiled by the Victorians, but the galleries and much ironwork suggest its original character. Christ Church is in pale yellow

brick and was designed in a sensible Early Pointed style by Thomas Smith of Madeley in 1838 (it is strongly reminiscent of his other church at Ironbridge), but much coloured glass makes it very dark inside. Wrekin College (formerly known as Wellington College) was founded in 1880 by John Bayley. On the Holy-

All Saints WELLINGTON, 1790

head Road is the *Old Hall*, now a school, of genuine half-timber. It was built in the fifteenth century as a residence for Keepers of the Wrekin. At *Arleston* is another half-timbered manor house. William Withering and Sarah Smith were two of Wellington's most illustrious citizens. Withering was an eighteenth century

141

physician, scientist, mineralogist and botanist of no mean standing and was one of the earliest advocates of the abolition of the slave trade. On hearing of his death, a contemporary wit remarked "the flower of the physicians is Withering". Sarah Smith, daughter of a local bookseller and postmaster, and better known under her pseudonym of Hesba Stretton, became a most successful writer of highly moral and best-selling novels. Her first, *Jessica's First Prayer*, published in 1866, sold 1½ million copies and became, in translation, a set book in Russian schools on the orders of the Czar. The ample proceeds from her writing enabled Miss Smith to travel widely and devote herself to good works. She helped to found the London Society for the Prevention of Cruelty to Children, and which later became the nucleus of the N.S.P.C.C. It is still possible to hire a horse-drawn carriage in Wellington!

Welshampton (5). The yellow stone church with diaper pattern slate roof was designed in thirteenth-century style by Sir Gilbert Scott. In a grave in the churchyard is buried Moshueshue, son of a Basuto chief who died in 1824 while studying at a missionary college. He is also depicted in a window in the church, robed in white, attended by a servant and chariot, being baptised, by a river.

Wem (5). Is an interesting little market town on the R. Roden in flat lands of the N. Shropshire plain. Its past is perhaps worthy of more note than its present, for it has an air of sad neglect about it; a plasterer's trowel and a paint brush could work wonders for the main street, as the beautifully maintained National Westminster Bank building shows. The castle has long since disappeared and most of the earlier buildings were destroyed in a Great Fire in 1677. During the Civil War, Wem was the first town in Shropshire to declare for Parliament and a garrison of forty soldiers, aided by townsfolk, repulsed a Royalist attempt on the town led by Lord Capel. *Richard Baxter*, the Puritan divine, helped

in its defence. After the Restoration, in 1685, the barony of Wem was sold by Daniel Wycherley to the notorious *Judge Jeffreys*, who took the title, Baron of Wem. Lowe Hall, his home for a time, bears the date 1666, but a new brick façade was added in the early nineteenth-century. *William Hazlitt* spent his boyhood here in Noble Street in what is now known as Hazlitt House. *John Astley*, society portrait painter and friend of Sir Joshua Reynolds, and *John Ireland*, biographer of Hogarth, were both born here. *William Henry Betty*, the child actor, also lived in the town for some time. The church has an old tower but is rather dull. Beside it is the former Market Hall, columned and arcaded, and in the other direction is the Town Hall, 1905, with Cheese Hall added in 1928. A Cheese Fair used to be held here on every third Wednesday. In New Street a garage utterly ruins the front of the Hall, a Georgian red brick house, and probably the best in the town. Altogether, a town which deserves far better treatment than it has received. *Soulton Hall*, two miles, is a very attractive Carolean house, 1668, altered later on but still with an impressive doorway.

Little Wenlock (12). A well-kept village high up under the craggy shoulder of the Wrekin. The older houses cluster round the church but there has been a lot of infilling with modern houses. The *Old Hall* is a remnant of an Elizabethan mansion, with mullioned and transomed stone windows and gables. The church is mainly 1865 with a tower of 1667 and pretty weather-vane. Inside there is white plaster contrasted with pink and blue, all lit by clear glass. The churchyard has some good but neglected iron tombs, doubtless to be swept away in the senseless mania for "tidiness". To the south are vast spoil-heaps from opencast mining.

Much Wenlock (12). "The only remarkable piece of scenery we met on our way to Wenlock" (from Shrewsbury) "was a lofty bank, known by the name of Wenlock-edge. We saw it at a distance, running like a long, black ridge, covered with wood, athwart the country . . .

when we had attained the summit, we had no descent on the other side; this long ridge being the slope only of one of those grand, natural terraces, by which one tract of country sometimes descends into another." This was William Gilpin, writing in 1809. He was not pleased with Wenlock Priory as an example of a picturesque ruin. "The ruins offend from being too detached. In their present state we consider them only as *studies*: if they had been connected to each other by fragments of old walls, and connected with the ground by a few heaps of rubbish, and a little adorned with wood, we should have considered them in a higher style, and looked at them as picturesque." Visitors are less nicely discriminating about ruins in these days and indeed, as Pevsner says, picturesque and architectural interests often conflict. Suffice it that the ruins are now entrusted to the care of the M.P.B.W. and are well maintained in the manner of an English country garden. The Priory of St Milburga was founded about 680 but after many vicissitudes became a Cluniac house. The remaining buildings are mainly E.E. but the finest parts are the late Norman interlaced arcading on the Chapter House wall and the tender carvings on the Lavatorium wall. Six masons are now engaged in the long-term restoration of the ruins, and Mansfield stone is being used to replace the crumbling local stone. Close by is the Prior's Lodge, c. 1500, the best building in the town and one of the best buildings of its period in the country. The house has a splendid two-storey gallery, "more glass than wall", with arches and mullions framed in Alveley sandstone and capped with a magnificent stone-slated roof. There are many such roofs in the town still, the stone coming from Hoar Edge, some four miles away. Much Wenlock is a sleepy huddle of limestone, mellow Georgian brick and half-timbered houses which have grown up round the Priory. Holy Trinity church is a red sandstone Norman building with a rather later tower over a good W. door. Other later work includes a two-storey south porch and fourteenth-century chancel chapel. The Guildhall is a charming half-timbered

WHITCHURCH

building supported on wooden posts and "reared . . . over the prison house" in two days in 1577. Inside are the panelled court-room and council chamber. The centre of the town is mainly limestone and timber, with Georgian and Victorian buildings at the extremities and post-war housing tucked away out of sight. There are several good inns—The Raven has a delightful iron sign—*Ashfield House*

was once one of them and Charles I lunched there en route to Bridgnorth in 1642. In front of *Tickwood Hall* (2½ miles), he conferred with the local gentry in the Audience Meadow in an effort to raise money and men in support of his cause. One cannot help but be aware of the lively tradition of stone working in this town, and on the climb up to Wenlock Edge (Gilpin certainly

understated the nature of the hills here), one can still see the remains of workings at the side of the road. The parish register bears tribute to one Walter Hancock, d. 1599, who was "a very skilful man in the art of masonry, in setting of plottes for buildings and performing of the same, ingravings in alebaster in other stone or playster, and divers other giftes that belong to that art, as doth appear in his workes which may be seen in divers parkes of England and Walles, most sumpteous buildings, most stately tombs, most curyous pictures. And to conclude, in all works he took in hand he hath lefte behind him longe lastinge monuments of skilful workmanship, and besides these qualities he had others whiche passed these: he was a most honest man, devout and zealous in religion, pitiful to the poore, and had the love and goodwill of all his honest neighbours." He built Condover, High Ercall, and the Old Market Hall, Shrewsbury.

Wentnor (10). A wild and windy village 850 ft. up on a spur of the Long Mynd between the E. Onny and Criftin Brook. There are wonderful views of unspoilt country—Shropshire as one always imagines it. The stone houses cluster together for shelter round the church, with colour washes and crumbling decay in abandoned farm buildings. The church is almost entirely 1885 but with a few Norman fragments. It is not remarkable in itself but has some fine memorial slabs to the Medlicott family hidden away in a corner.

Westbury (7). The rounded tops of the Breidden Hills dominate the landscape here. The simple eighteenth-century tower with outside stair is more impressive than the scraped and spoiled interior of the church. The remnants of Caus Castle, border stronghold of the FitzCorbets, are nearby. The castle was finally destroyed during the Civil War.

Weston-under-Redcastle (5). On the S.W. edge of the Hawkstone estate, Weston is a pretty village. The church was built in 1791 but has since been severely gothicised, except for the tower which has a parapet. The village stocks still stand below the

WELLINGTON

churchyard wall. The *Hawkstone Park Hotel* is a well preserved Georgian stuccoed house with long Venetian windows opening out to the garden and semi-circular windows above.

Weston Lullingfields (8). A hamlet in the meadows near Baschurch. Gothic Revival church by Haycock Jnr., 1857, stands behind a screen of trees and in splendid isolation. An unstartling exterior but the inside is reminiscent of Holland; the walls are entirely white, set off by the dark-stained pews and a touch of colour in the arms painted on the corbels. The W. end is very fine with bare wires, weights and ropes of the clock mechanism against the whitewashed wall. A half-timbered passage links the church to the vicarage.

Stanwardine Hall. An Elizabethan house reputedly built by Robert Corbet and with a date of 1588.

Weston Rhyn (4). Uninspiring church in E.E. style, 1878. *The Quinta* is a lavish, castellated early nineteenth-century house with extensive shrubberies. On a grassy hill in the park, a Victorian copy of Stonehenge. *Moreton Hall*. one mile to the east, is a seventeenth-century brick house, now a girls' school.

Wheathill (4). Surrounded by hills and among hillocks lies the small Victorianised church with its high, narrow Norman doorway with rough hewn tympanum above. The original chancel arch remains with its moulding and carved capitals and there is a good seventeenth-century nave roof.

Whitchurch (5). Undoubtedly the most handsome town in north Shropshire, yet too often by-passed by the traveller to Wales or the North. Perhaps this is why the centre has remained comparatively unspoilt and keeps its character as a busy and thriving market town. As always, there are too many traffic signs, and this town would present an excellent opportunity for the Civic Trust to guide and advise on its preservation. But take a walk round the town at night. All its shortcomings are then concealed in the shadows; the amber sodium light and flood-lighting of the church accord well with the smoky sandstone of the church tower, and cosy pubs glow invitingly from yards and alleys. The finest building in Whitchurch is St Alkmund's church and, fittingly, it has the finest position, at the top of a hill, with Georgian almshouses and Elizabethan style school falling away to the north and the High Street climbing to meet it on the other side. The church was built in 1712–13 by William Smith with a grand and imposing sandstone tower dominating the town. It replaces an earlier building which fell down, after evensong, one Sunday in 1711. The semi-circular porch was rebuilt in 1925 after the original design, no doubt, a result of Wren's influence. The interior was much altered by unsympathetic ministrations during the last century and darkened by the addition of stained glass of little merit. However, the galleries remain and the Tuscan columns and arches and the coved ceiling are enough to show what a magnificent interior this must have been in the eighteenth century. The sumptuous organ case with cherubs' heads and trumpeting angel (early eighteenth century) has been moved but still delights. St Alkmund's contains what Hare called "the most important sepulchural monument in Shropshire"—the effigy of John Talbot, first Earl of Shrewsbury

". . . The scourge of France!
The Talbot so much fear'd abroad
That with his name, the mothers
     still'd their babes."
     (Shakespeare Henry VI)

After a glorious career in France, where he was captured but ransomed after four years captivity, he became Marshal of France, Earl of Shrewsbury, Lord Lieutenant of Ireland, Earl of Waterford and Wexford and, finally, Lord Lieutenant of Aquitaine. At the end, this octogenerian warrior was killed, with his son, at Chatillon near Bordeaux in 1453. His bones and heart lie here in his native Whitchurch. Down the hill, in High Street, are two fine banks—the National Westminster is timber-framed, a former inn and incorporating the doors of the old church, while opposite, Barclays occupies what was once the Market Hall. Close by is a complete cast-iron shop front three storeys high and well maintained. From the churchyard another street, St Mary's, leads down the hill in a series of Georgian houses, each with its own delightful variation on the theme of a classical doorway. At the bend is a former Methodist chapel, 1810, with arched windows and pediment, now the post office, and near the Trustee Savings Bank, 1846, is the pub where Sir Edward German was born. Whitchurch and *Dodington* now lie cheek by jowl and the latter boasts a handsome Greek revival church, 1836, St Catherine's, with pleasant late-Georgian or early-Victorian stucco houses opposite. *Whitchurch* was once famed for its cheese-making, but the long-established church clock-making and engineering industries still flourish. Randolph Caldecott, the illustrator of nursery rhymes, was a clerk in the Whitchurch and Ellesmere Bank.

Whittington (4). A main-road village passed through by thousands on their way to N. Wales and the mountains. The castle is a picturesque ruin, half surrounded by a moat and guarded by an impressive gateway with two round towers. It is seen at its best at night, floodlit. The church is in red brick with a tower of 1747. The promising Georgian nave, 1804, by Harrison, is belied by the Lombardesque tracery of the windows and the cap on the tower. This and the sumptuous interior work in a similar style is the consequence of the "improvements" of 1894. William Walsham How was rector here for 28 years and poetically scolded the former rector and the architect, Harrison:

"Nevertheless the church you
     gave us
Ugly is past all comparison
O you dreadful Mr Harrison."

W. W. How later became Bishop How ("For all the saints who from their labours rest", "Summer suns are glowing"), and it was in his memory that much of the later enrichment was carried out. There is an interesting east Jesse window by F. C. Eden, 1934.

Whitton (17). This is red sandstone country and the parent rock gives

colour to the fertile soil, making the district reminiscent of Devon. Winding high-banked lanes lead down from the Ludlow-Cleobury Mortimer road, across little hills, through a magnificent patchwork of fields and hedges, the Abberley Hills and the Malverns forming a misty blue backdrop to the scene. Whitton village is a small collection of black and white houses with a sprinkling of stone and newer brick. The long, low church stands aloof from the village on a hill slope; the nave and chancel are Norman, but Sir Aston Webb extended the chancel in 1891 and the Morris and Burne Jones E. window dates from about this time. An open framed porch protects the original Norman doorway and the squat fourteenth-century tower completes the composition. *Whitton Court* has an E-shaped front in Elizabethan brick, a partial refacing of a fourteenth-century stone hall, with further alterations dating from 1682. It looks out, over attractive lawns and planting, to a small but handsome park and the Herefordshire hills beyond.

Whixall (5). Large and scattered parish in the far north of the county adjoining the Flintshire border. Close by is an extensive tract of peat known as Whixall Moss, the layers of which are 7–8 feet thick and dangerously boggy in places. This is still cut and dried in the neighbourhood but is mainly used for horticultural purposes. Large areas have been denuded, drained and reclaimed for farming. The plain red brick and stone church was built by G. E. Street in 1867 and has an exposed brick interior. *Bostock Hall*, at a crossroads to the west of the village, is a small seventeenth-century brick farmhouse with a charming garden. Part of the Shropshire Union Canal is cut along the harder edge of the Moss.

Willey (12). Deep among woodlands which are the remnants of the ancient Forest of Shirlett, the village is surrounded by gentle slopes dotted with mature beech, chestnut and fir. The only remains of the Old Hall are two stone stable ranges with gables

◁ WHITCHURCH

WILLEY Old Hall

and mullioned windows. A few solid retainers' cottages with pretty gardens lie close by. The church has a battlemented eighteenth-century tower with arched windows, but Sir Arthur Blomfield virtually rebuilt the Norman nave and chancel in 1880 and the interior is scraped and rather gloomy. In the churchyard a tombstone records that a lady who died in 1756 at the age of 113 "danced with the Morris dancers the year before".

The old village of Willey which stood on a slope to the N.E. of Willey Hall was entirely removed to provide greater privacy for the Forrester family when their new house was built about 1815 to replace the Old Hall. The architect of Willey Park was Lewis Wyatt and his classical design is elegant and superbly sited in a splendid landscape, overlooking a series of lakes.

It is hard to realise that this now essentially rural area was once a hub of activity in the Shropshire iron industry and hence of the Industrial Revolution. Just down the road, beside the brook, stood Willey Old Furnace, while on the Broseley road was the New Furnace, leased in 1757 to John Wilkinson. Here was set up one of the first Boulton and Watt steam engines, installed under the personal supervision of James Watt, and here Wilkinson developed his new process for boring cannon and thus established his fame and fortune. Later on, at Willey wharf on the Severn, he launched *The Trial*, the world's first iron boat.

Wistanstow (14). A secluded village on rolling foothills at the southern end of Ape Dale and Wenlock Edge. From here, roads fan out into the Dale and up to Church Stretton, under the Long Mynd. The name is taken from St Wystan, thought to be the rightful king of Mercia, but who refused the crown to devote himself to the religious life and was treacherously slain by a jealous cousin. This is a mainly stone village with some thatched black and white houses. Behind the church is an elegant nineteenth-century school with white-painted round-headed windows set in warm grey sandstone. Just below are some Gothic iron gates and posts of the same period. The church dates from about 1200 and Dean Cranage judged the N. transept roof to be of this period; it is certainly in remarkably good condition. The nave roof, on the other hand, is of 1630 with typical Shropshire quatrefoil windbraces with white-painted plaster between and gilded carving on the bosses. The walls have been scraped but the box-pews (1801) remain and still bear their family names. In the S. transept are some seventeenth-century Commandments, Creed and Lord's Prayer in ornamental frames. Outside are some singularly delicate eighteenth- and nineteenth-century lettering and carving on the churchyard head-stones.

Cheney Longville. Dipping and swooping valleys with well-wooded slopes lead to this little village of romantic name. The ruins of a moated and fortified manor house besieged during the Civil War are now incorporated in a farm. The landscape here can scarcely have changed over the past five hundred years.

Withington (8). A homely village by the Shropshire Union, in a flat fertile district reminiscent of Holland. The dark sandstone church by the canal is by G. E. Street, 1874, but lacks the sparkle of his touch at Upton Magna. There is a stone re-redos and pulpit and in the tower a brass to Adam Grafton, a great pluralist, d. 1530. He was Rector of Albright Hussey, Withington, and Upton Magna; Master of Battlefield College; Canon of St Chad's, Shrewsbury . . . Chaplain to Edward V and Prince Arthur, "the most worshipful priest lyvying in hys days." Behind the church is a mellow red brick late seventeenth-century house. Nearby, at Allscott, is a sugar beet factory.

Wollaston (7). Background of Breidden Hills. The red brick church is 1788, but Victorian restoration has removed most of its classic dignity. The cottage of *Old Parr*, Shropshire's super-centenarian, is at *Glyn*, not far from here. Reputed to have been 152 years old when he died, he had the distinction of being buried in Westminster Abbey. A brass plate, engraved with his portrait, in Wollaston church, describes him as "The Old, Old, very Old Man, Thomas Parr". Although there is no evidence to support the legend, his feats certainly appear to have been beyond most men! He never lost his zest for life, first married at 80, fathering two children, and for the second time at 120, fathering another child. His ordinary diet is said to have consisted of rancid cheese, milk, coarse hard bread, and small drink, generally whey. At 145 he threshed corn and accom-

plished the daily farm work. Brought on a litter, by easy stages, to London to meet the king and see the sights, this old rogue quickly became the talk of the town and one of the sights himself. But the rich diet and excitement were too much for the ancient rustic, and he soon succumbed.

Wombridge (9). Part of Oakengates, with a church of 1869, by S. Bidlake of Birmingham.

Woodcote (9). On the main Newport road out of Tong and about midway between the two. The road skirts the park where Cockerell built the fanciful red brick Hall in 1875; in Jacobean-Georgian with Byzantine embellishments, it must surely have been inspired by the exotic Tong Castle. It is now a school and the park has suffered a change leaving the house looking rather isolated. Behind, and alongside the new Roman Catholic chapel, is the Norman church, much renewed but with monuments to the Cotes' family stretching from 1485 to 1898.

Woolstaston (11). In a pretty situation at the N. end of the Long Mynd and looking across to Caer Caradoc. There are many half-timber houses round the village green with some old work in the Hall, near the church, which has a black and white porch in keeping. The modern carving in the pulpit and elsewhere was paid for "from the proceeds of a booklet, 'A Night in the Snow', describing the wonderful escape of the late rector, Edmund Donald Carr, on a tempestuous night of 29 January, 1865. Returning from taking a service at Ratlinghope, he lost his way on the Long Mynd, and wandered for 27 hours, with great difficulty escaping with his life." (Rev. J. E. Auden.) The carving is the work of a local craftsman.

Woolston (see West Felton).

Woore (6). On the old London-to-Chester road, in the corner of the county where it meets Cheshire and Staffordshire, and not far from Stoke-on-Trent. A large and straggling village with a racecourse for the annual Hunt Steeplechases and hurdle races. The classic church, 1830, still has an

air of distinction and individuality despite repair, renovation, rebuilding and reseating over the past 140 years. Its crisp white lines make a welcome contrast to the usual sandstone building and these are echoed by the contemporary façade of the Swan Hotel opposite. This is much older, beneath the plaster, dating back to the fifteenth-century.

Worfield (12). This parish is one of the largest in England to be served by a single church and comprises some thirty hamlets, all of which were mentioned in the Domesday survey. The large church is set beneath a wooded slope; its tall, slender spire is a landmark for miles around. This is of most elegant proportions and springs from a handsome late fourteenth-century tower in red sandstone. The rest of the building is thirteenth and fourteenth century, almost certainly on the site of a much earlier structure, with a floor sloping down from the W. towards the E. window. There are two good alabaster tombs of the Bromley family, sixteenth and seventeenth century, the latter with a six-poster canopy above. The Victorian restoration swept away the eighteenth-century porch and was, as usual, far too thorough. By the churchyard gates stands the former *Worfield Grammar School*, a diminutive black and white house, and opposite is *Lower House*. This is a fine half-timbered house with a gabled façade; the eighteenth-century alterations and the recent restoration make this a worthy foil to the church in the centre of the village.

On the outskirts is *Davenport House*, standing in a well-landscaped park with a round dovecote with a lantern, all on a little knoll. This handsome house is of red brick and stone and was built by Francis Smith of Warwick in 1726 (cf. Mawley Hall.). At *Chesterton*, two miles away, the only remains of the former fifteenth-century chapel are a Perp. doorway and some windows. Nearby cottages are reputed to have been built from its stones. *Chesterton Farm* is a large, pleasant, early eighteenth-century red brick house with a hipped roof and the perfect examplar for the between-the-wars Georgian Revival. *Ewdness Manor*

House has big sixteenth-century brick star-shaped chimney stacks rising above stone walls. *Swancote Farm* is late eighteenth-century brick with a square summer-house with dovecote, above, topped by a pyramid roof.

Worthen (10). A large stone-built village halfway between Shrewsbury and Montgomery, in the Rea valley. The church, set back from the road, has a short, sturdy tower. A pretty timber and red brick seventeenth-century porch with balustraded sides protects a fourteenth-century doorway. Inside the nave walls have been scraped and Victorian glass keeps out most of the light. The woodwork is most striking: three long lines of seats with bobbin ends, Elizabethan benches and Jacobean box-pews,

with a coat of arms on the Squire's, nearest the two-decker pulpit. *Hampton Hall* is an isolated seventeenth-century red brick mansion at Leigh, on the foothills of Long Mountain. It looks across to the Stiperstones with a big stone porch with curly-arched pediment (1749).

Wrockwardine (9). Now a residential village for Wellington and Oakengates, with many villa residences. The best approach is with the Wrekin at one's back, when farms and barns make a strong silhouette on the skyline. The church is mainly Victorian but is better than many, with its narrow nave and very broad chancel and transepts; most was originally late twelfth century. The octagonal Jacobean pulpit is very elaborately carved and there is a splen-

did Rococo memorial tablet to Wm. Cludde, d. 1765, with cherubs, scrolls, urn and painted shield. *Wrockwardine Hall*, with its Georgian front and hipped roof, lies behind and below the church. It is part Georgian and part seventeenth century. *Wrockwardine Wood*, near Oakengates, has a red brick church by Thomas Smith of Madeley, 1833, modernised by Gilbert Scott in 1889. A coalmining district. *Admaston*, nearby, enjoyed a fashionable popularity as a spa in the nineteenth century but is now almost forgotten. There are two wells, one sulphurous, the other chalybeate. In 1851 there was an "hotel and boarding house . . . a handsome pile greatly admired for its architectural beauty, erected at a cost of £6,000". The spa was in the grounds of the Clock House.

At WORFIELD

△ Iron Porch at WROCKWARDINE

Wroxeter (11). Uriconium: once a Roman town of great importance, flourishing in the first and second centuries A.D. and now celebrated for its ruins. A large proportion of the finds here are in Rowley's House Museum, Shrewsbury, but others are exhibited at the site (M.P.B.W.). The ugly green-painted corrugated-iron huts are, unfortunately more obvious than the ruins themselves. The church, close by, is grossly neglected and deserves far better treatment. Its present state is disgraceful: the walls and floor ooze with moisture, windows are broken and hatchments hang in tatters. The interior represents every style from the Norman to the Victorian. In the chancel are four really fine monuments with beautiful colouring; the communion rail is dated 1637 and the pulpit and box-pews are Jacobean. The nave and south aisle were put under one roof in the eighteenth-century with a flat ceiling. The enormous font, well placed in a wide nave, was probably hewn out of the base of a Roman column by its Norman carver. The stained glass E. window with the twelve Apostles is perhaps by Evans of Shrewsbury. Apart from its neglect, this large village church remains unspoilt by the hands of the "restorers" and "improvers", and even has its rough, irregular brick floor in the nave. Outside, in the S. wall, is part of a Saxon cross with interlace carving and a dragon. The churchyard gate is fashioned from rough Roman columns and capitals and others form a grotto in a neighbouring garden.

Wyre Forest (15). This is mainly in Worcestershire but stretches between Bewdley and Cleobury on both sides of the Severn. This is what remains of a much larger, ancient forest as at Clun, Dartmoor and Exmoor but plenty remains to make this the New Forest of the West Midlands, a veritable picknickers' paradise. There are scrub oaks, larch and pine with bracken and heather thriving on the clay soil, all carefully tended by the Forestry Commission.

Yockleton (8) A main-road hamlet. The nineteenth-century church by Haycock has a tall thin spire and rather incongruous dormer windows.

Roman inscription in WROXETER museum ▷

150

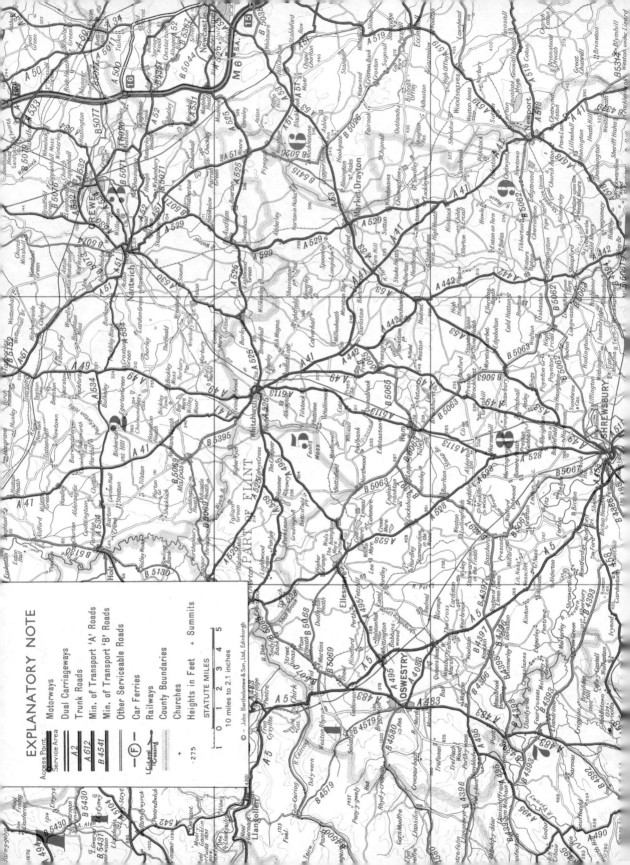

EXPLANATORY NOTE

Access Point	Motorways
Service Area	Dual Carriageways
A2	Trunk Roads
A612	Min. of Transport 'A' Roads
B4541	Min. of Transport 'B' Roads
	Other Serviceable Roads
	Car Ferries
	Railways
—(F)—	County Boundaries
Level Crossing	Churches
∙275	Heights in Feet ▲ Summits

STATUTE MILES

1   0   1   2   3   4   5

10 miles to 2.1 inches

© — John Bartholomew & Son, Ltd., Edinburgh

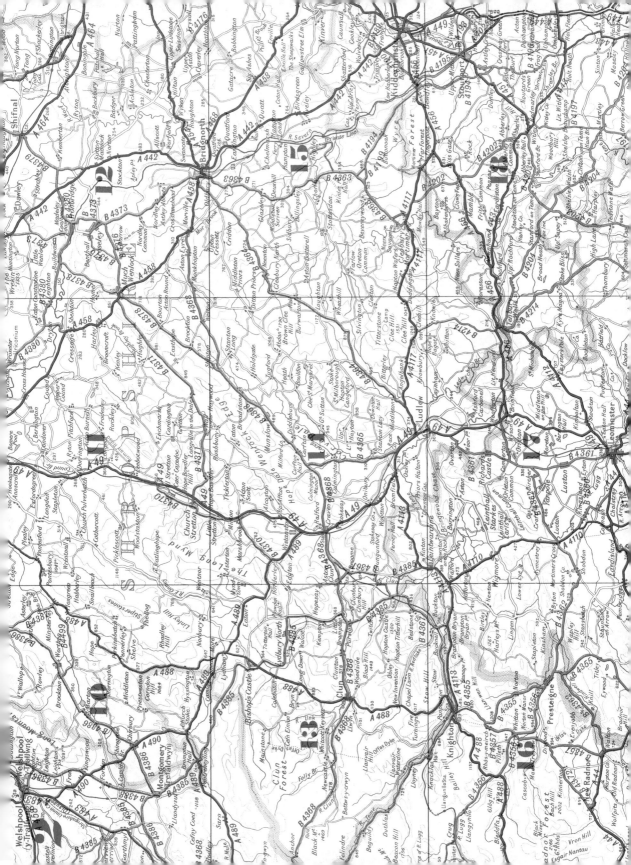

Index

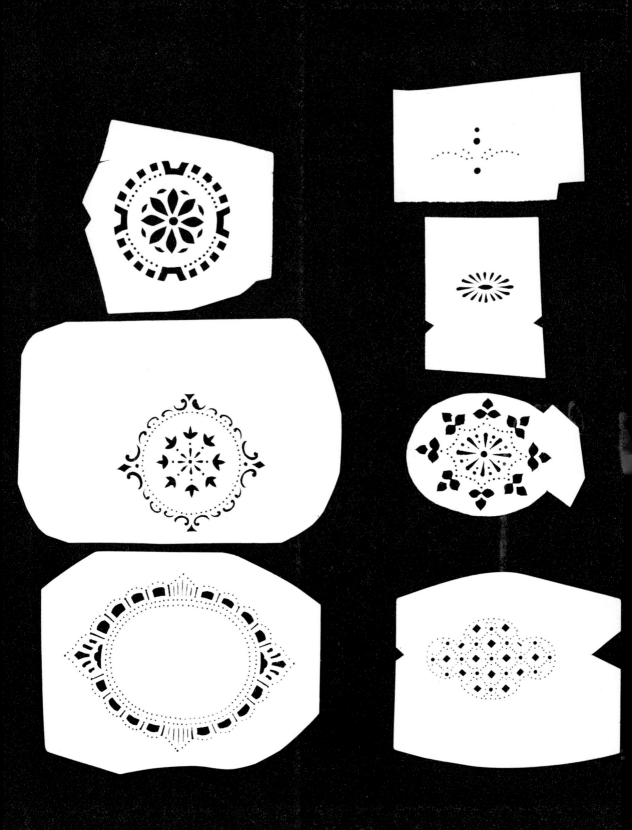